The Spirit With

Evelyn Capel

The Spirit Within Us

Floris Books

Edited by Tom Ravetz

First published privately in the 1950s
This edition published in 2010 by Floris Books

British Library CIP Data available

ISBN 978-086315-748-6

Printed in Great Britain
by Bell & Bain, Glasgow

Contents

Foreword

Evelyn Capel (1911–2000) was born at Stow-on-the-Wold in the Cotswold Hills in England. She studied history at Somerville College, Oxford, and then studied at the seminary of The Christian Community in Stuttgart. In 1939, she became the first English woman priest ordained within it to celebrate the sacraments. She held numerous courses on a wide variety of subjects, on which she also wrote. Two of her most central concerns are represented by the two parts of this book: the cultivation on an inner life in a Christian sense, drawing on the insights of Rudolf Steiner; and the development of freedom in thought and deed, as outlined in Steiner's *Philosophy of Spiritual Activity*.

The chapters of this book were written as letters to members and friends of The Christian Community in the mid 1950s. They contain the content of courses that she held over many years. When I was a newly-ordained priest in Aberdeen in the mid 1990s, I experienced Evelyn's course on *The Philosophy of Spiritual Activity*, forty years after these letters were written, when Evelyn was well into her eighties. Although by then her delivery had slowed a little, the breadth of interest, the resolutely non-churchy tone, and the deep devotion that informed her work were still strongly to be experienced.

The founders of The Christian Community were in no doubt that their task was far wider than renewal of the church, or of a religious life understood as separate from the life of the world. One of the earliest publications of the young movement was a series of booklets entitled *Christus aller Erde* or

Christ of the whole earth. It was clear to them that the task of renewing culture and society which they felt had a unique source of help in the work of Rudolf Steiner. It has been important in the intervening years to be clear about what is the specific task of religious renewal, and what is that of the anthroposophical movement — not least because souls who find their way more easily to one movement or the other, and their access is not helped if the two seem to merge. However, this book can remind us how for Evelyn there was no division. It was typical of her understanding of the world that she called her course on *The Philosophy of Spiritual Activity,* 'The Working of the Holy Spirit.' The most philosophical of Steiner's works, which contains hardly a reference to Christian dogma, is revealed to be a workbook for experiencing the Holy Spirit at work. When we become clear about what happens when we truly know, then — to paraphrase the Trinity epistle of the Act of Consecration of Man — we experience the Spirit receiving our knowing into his life.

Tom Ravetz

Part I

Thoughts on the Inner Life

1

Awakening to our Potential

At the outset a word of explanation should be given about the point of view from which these thoughts on the inner life are put together. Not long ago an advertisement in an underground station caught my eye. Its heading was: 'Let me show you the man you can become.' Underneath was the picture of a man bulging in every limb with muscles, which he had acquired by the use of certain apparatus for physical exercises. The motto seemed to me right, too great in fact for the end it served. In many other ways, people can be observed looking for the person they can become. There are any number of courses and classes offering lessons in self-development, or in learning new skills. This is a sign of an awareness that in the sphere of the soul, in the life of the spirit, there is more that we can become. The activity of the inner life is the means of growing and developing the man of spirit within, who is there in every one of us, but who has not yet become that which he can become.

There are some people for whom the inner life means a path of esoteric development in the course of which they learn to be conscious of and cultivate special faculties. It is not within the scope of these pages to speak of this. Teaching on this subject is available and can be sought elsewhere by anyone who feels called upon to do so. But this is not the only form of active inner life that is necessary today.

How many people today find themselves in situations in life with which they do not know how to cope. How often do we not have to make decisions for which we feel that we have not enough wisdom? How often do we not meet overwhelming experiences? How often do we not feel, if only I could be wiser, greater of heart, more courageous to meet the events, the people, the problems, the decisions that come upon me? It is part of the destiny of our time that we have to find our strength from within ourselves. This cannot be done all at once or by wishing for it. There is however a source of strength within each one of us. It is the gift of Christ to human souls. It can be found, developed and taken up into consciousness by an active inner life. Doing this needs thought and care. The thoughts in these pages are intended to be a contribution to this problem which meets us all through life itself.

From the point of view that is to be the starting point here the inner life means the care of the 'man within,' who is there in everyone, but who can only become what he can be through spiritual effort within the soul. Those who do not give attention and thought to the 'man within' are not really living a full human life. They are leaving out a part of their whole existence. Those who give such attention are few today compared with those who do not, but it is all the more necessary that they should be awake to the importance and the needs of the 'man within.'

Let us look a little further at the fact that we, as human beings, have something within us that requires development. How does this come about? It is not difficult to observe that in the world in which we live as human beings, we are different from the creatures around us. Stones, plants and animals have already become what they are destined to be. The changes they pass through in the course of their existence are limited to the laws of their nature, which they have no urge to surpass. What is specially characteristic of the human being is the conviction that we are not yet finished and fulfilled, that we have still to become something. In the nature of our bodies we have something in common with the other creatures. Our bodies have their own laws of existence and we can only change them up to a point and indirectly. Once upon a time in the far distant past divine beings meditated the form and shape of the human being into creation. Through long ages of evolution the form took on little by little bodily substance and became the earthly image for the thought of the gods. Everyone bears the impress of the divine idea in their body, not by their own doing or making, but by a divine gift.

The human form divine is the mark of our humanity but by virtue of it the body is more human than the soul. The chaotic life of thought, feeling and will is a less perfect mirror of the image of God than is the harmonious form of the body. In the impulses of the soul, we meet what is unshaped and unfinished in ourselves and therein we find the opportunity for becoming through our own effort. The form of the body is a divine gift, which we accept from beyond ourselves. In the soul we find the sphere in which we ourselves can directly work and have a hand in the completion of our humanity.

The creative power of soul, which we can find within ourselves, comes from Christ. From him likewise is the idea and the pattern of the new man, who should grow from within. Christ came into the world to bring to the lost souls of people the idea of what the human being could still become. Without his coming, all thought of what it means to be human would long have been forgotten. Before Christ came, when people sought to find the idea of their humanity, they had to look into the past. They strove to behold the beginnings of humankind, the image of man as created by the will of God. Those who worshipped their ancestors did so because each forefather, the further back he had lived, was nearer to the divine image of the creation. Since Christ came, we look forward to find the ideal of our humanity. We seek it in that which we still have to become. The being of Christ reveals to us the picture and substance of this ideal. We know in him that which we strive to attain and we find in him the helper in our striving. To recognize the 'man within' and the need for his becoming is to find the working of Christ in the heart.

Everyone is capable of an active inner life in this sense but
not everyone recognizes this. There is therefore a natural distinction between those who are interested in it and those who
are not. Those who have this interest find the problem before
them of how in practice to set about this task. My intention in
these pages is simply to gather from the work of Rudolf
Steiner some advice and teaching on how to care for the life of
the soul so that one may grow in spirit and in likeness to the
ideal of Christ, which is the aim of man's becoming. Should
anyone feel that in working at his own inner life, he might be
in danger of thinking too much of himself, there is comfort in
the thought that he is aiming at something which is not just for
his own sake. There is a danger of selfishness in wanting to be
more advanced than other people, in order to know more and
have more authority. There is no such danger in aiming with
one's efforts at coming nearer in one's whole being to the ideal
of man. To this end effort is rightly used on one's self, for
developing one's own nature will help others in their struggle
of becoming. Another danger arises only if one begins to
believe in changing others, instead of changing one's self and
one's own life.

It might seem to be one of the attractions of the inner life
that it is often the interest of only a few special people. Some of
the charm is perhaps lost by starting from the bold conviction
that it is essential to human nature to wish for the fulfilment of
one's own humanity. But there is in reality no problem here.
There is something special in realizing consciously what is
meant by the task of being human. A vision of the mind and
heart is needed to see this and the seers may well seem few
compared with those who do not see. But in a Christian sense,
those who see will not be anxious to keep the vision to themselves. Christ has brought into our world the ideal of what
man shall become and it should shine forth for all human
souls just as the sun shines for all humankind.

Nevertheless there is a particular responsibility in being
aware of these things. I remember once walking one Sunday

afternoon in spring across Hyde Park. There were hundreds of people sitting, walking or running on the grass. Each one was busy with his holiday, with the sunny pause in his daily round and with the struggle of his destiny. Each one was assuming that the meaning of his existence was summed up in his own affairs. However, observing as I was able to do at that moment, a large crowd of people in relaxation, the other side of existence made itself felt. I began to realize that those people were in their souls open to the heavens, that they were in the field in which the angels and all the company of the divine world cultivate the evolution and destiny of man. These souls were not opposing the work of God in themselves, but they were preoccupied and unaware. They were behaving as if all this side of existence were not their business. But it is our business and in our time, more than ever before, souls need to awake to this realization. Those who awaken feel a growing responsibility as their awareness develops.

Am I fitted for this kind of responsibility? Are there not other people, more advanced, better read, better able to think, in much more favourable circumstances than myself? Such a doubt assails many of us. It is caused by an attitude of mind that is powerful in the social life of today, in which we are all naturally involved. People are so frequently estimated by what they have achieved or by what they can show in position, wealth, etc. The whole system of testing and examinations causes people to rely on what they have attained, which becomes their identity. In spiritual matters such an attitude is without value. Here the test should be: what am I aiming at, to what shall I devote myself? Not something out of the past, but the strength of the future, if the ideal to be served is important. In the Revelation to St John a certain group of people is described as 'the saints.' They are the followers of Christ and on a quick reading one might assume that these are the souls who have achieved the Christian ideal in themselves. But in reality they are not the people who have already achieved something. They are those with enthusiasm for the aims and ideals which are revealed in Christ. They are called to be saints through their vision of what is to come, by their devotion to the task of the future.

What then are the means to an active inner life in this sense? There is a very common preconception that comes from history, that people really devoted to such interests must change their way of living and withdraw from the world. In the Middle Ages, for instance, there was a double order of society, the sacred and the secular, and most people had to decide between two ways of life, between activity turned outwards and activity turned inwards. This state of affairs should not persist today. Rudolf Steiner has shown a way of inner life which belongs to modern times and to modern consciousness. It can be fitted into our ordinary way of living by anyone who arranges his affairs in good order. There is also nothing about Steiner's suggestions that would tend to make anyone who follows them into an extraordinary or odd sort of person. It is rather like this: self-respecting people feel that they need a certain order and behaviour in daily life. They can see the advantages of good habits of cleanliness, regular meals and the right amount of sleep. They usually feel better if the rooms they inhabit are cared for, if their finances are in control. It is a bad sign for the health of a person if he begins to look uncared for and untidy. It is a moving experience to observe sometimes in bus, underground or crowded street, how well such masses of people have cared for their appearance, whatever their circumstances may be.

In this sphere there is a widespread awareness that a we are not 'finished' without our own effort, that we need constantly to do something to ourselves in order to look human. This all depends on daily custom. The inner life is only an extension of this kind of effort to the inner affairs of the soul. There is such a thing as a cultivated life of the soul, as well as a cultivated appearance. It is part of what I can do to make something of myself in the course of my daily life.

Once upon a time, in the old Celtic form of Christianity,

the cultivation of the soul in a Christian sense was understood and valued as much as the tilling of the land and the sailing of the seas. Many people chose then to live an orderly life, in which the order proceeded from the church. Discipline was regulated by the ringing of the bell and the singing of liturgies in accordance with the hours of the day and the alternation of work and prayer. Nowadays such an arrangement from outside does not accord with the development of individual responsibility. It would not be good to lay down a rule of life or to make regulations that were the same for everyone. Each person has to take the cultivation of their own soul-life in hand, within the limits of their circumstances, just as they care for their bodily life. There are nevertheless guiding ideas that are true and right for people living in our own time, which can be practised according to the individual judgment of each one. The best of these are to be found in the works of Rudolf Steiner.

We, ourselves, as we are, with our human faculties and customs are, so to speak, the material for the practice of the inner life. Let us think for a moment of the fact that we spend part of our existence awake and part asleep. We arrange for this as a matter of course in our outer affairs. We provide ourselves with beds to sleep in and other furniture for the things we do when we are awake. Our time is also divided between these two states. We know that we have to pass from one to another and back again. Some people find this easy, others difficult. Falling asleep has become a great problem for many. This is often due to the one-sided use of the human forces, which conditions today make seemingly inevitable. Generally speaking, it is true to say that people are kept awake by forces that they have not used in the daytime, while they may have over-used other forces. A good help is to take care that head, heart and hands have all been used during the day. People who work in offices can be greatly helped by an artistic activity, perhaps doing eurythmy. Those tied to a household might choose deliberately to read about cosmic events and historical happenings. There are a variety of possible examples. Waking up has also its problems for many people. It is certainly important to wake up thoroughly in the daytime and to go to sleep thoroughly at night. This produces a healthy balance in the soul.

Sleeping and waking are important processes for the spiritual life. In sleep the self and the soul pass into the spiritual world while the body is being refreshed. Some people are blessed with dreams, which reflect something of the spiritual experience of sleep. Many dreams are reflections of earthly experience, for instance the state of health. But beyond this, indications of the spiritual state of the soul or even of cosmic events are often woven into the picture language of dreams. Dreams need careful reading and their pictures are only a kind of language. Almost more important than dreams are the two transitions from waking to sleeping and from sleeping to waking. To prepare properly for sleep is part of a cared for, tidy inner life. The experiences of the daytime need to be put aside (there is a special exercise for doing this) and the mind and heart turned towards the world of the spirit. This is a very good time for prayer and meditation. Waking up is likewise an important moment. It is not helpful to force the soul too quickly back into the body, by hurrying the process. Rudolf Steiner advised people not to look straight at the light on waking, but to stay in twilight for a while. 'Daily dozens' and cold baths are still more violent methods of forcing a quick incarnation. In the slower process of waking, the mind has more chance to gather up the wisdom that is given by the world of spirit in sleep. More can be carried from the night into the day.

The greatest mystery of sleeping and waking lies in the activity of Christ. By day we are free to cultivate our thoughts, to grasp spiritual ideas and to wish to turn them into ideals. Yet we have not the power, as we may often notice, to carry these spiritual thoughts directly into our will. To become our ideal self is beyond our human power. Christ comes to our aid and in the time of sleep turns thought into will, idea into living ideal. Each time we sleep, we are again offering our thoughts to Christ that he may transform them for us into will. The simple daily event of sleeping and waking is of great spiritual importance. It can be the starting-point for the cultivation of an active inner life.

2

Sleeping and Waking

Falling asleep and waking up are the crossing of a frontier. The frontier lies between the world of earth, where we live in the body and have a wakeful consciousness, and the world of the spirit, into which the soul and the self withdraw in sleep and where our consciousness is either very dim or ceases altogether. Our existence as human beings belongs to both worlds, for it includes both states of sleeping and waking. We are not only the product of what happens to us and what we do when we are awake and conscious. We owe just as much to that which happens to us when we are asleep and unconscious. The frontier between two worlds across which our souls come and go is the same as the one over which we have to pass at birth and again at death. Then we have to do with the whole of our being what we do in part every time we sleep. The frontier is the same, but our experience of it is different.

We have already seen that this transition from one world to another, which most of us make every night, is an important element in the inner life. Now we will look at this matter in greater detail. We are accustomed to regard going to sleep as passing from consciousness to unconsciousness. In our waking hours, each of us is aware of ourselves, of our way of living, our destiny, our troubles and problems, of our actions and intentions. When we wake up in the morning, we are aware of returning to all these things. When the soul and the self leave the body, they lose the basis for our ordinary consciousness. They go into oblivion, being bereft of the body, which, during the hours of wakefulness, mirrors their experiences and thereby makes them conscious. This oblivion, though it seems dark to our conscious minds, is in reality filled with experience, though of a different kind from that of the daytime. It is experience, not of ourselves, but of the world. Free of the body, free of the limitations of the personality, the soul soars into the widths of the spirit and participates in the life of the world. By day our souls are occupied with self-interest, by night with world-interest.

The dreams, which come to us in the darkness of sleep, sometimes reflect this world-interest, but not always. Many dreams speak about something in ourselves and yet even these have a different aspect from that of waking life. They can give us a glimpse of the world-interest that absorbs us in sleep, if we are able to read them aright. The part of a dream that attracts our attention is the succession of vivid, quickly changing pictures. They are so often a pleasant escape from the limitations of ordinary life. Some people fly through the air in their dreams, appear in glorious clothes or travel to other lands or periods of history. Such pictures are fascinating but they are in fact the less important part of our dreams. They are usually pictures of what lies in our own psychological make-up. The significant part is to be found in the action, the drama that takes place. For instance, someone who is in great difficulties in his life may dream that he has to make a violent effort. That is significant, but it is less important whether this effort is expressed in the picture of climbing a steep slope, wading through deep water or lifting a heavy weight.

When we remember a dream and direct our attention to its action something valuable appears. We may see an event in life or a state of soul more clearly described than in our waking thoughts. We see something of ourselves, but the angle is different. We see from outside and from the distance something that in our waking thoughts we could only see from inside, tangled up with our emotions. In this way dreams, even if they speak of ourselves, can be helpful messages from another sphere. The following example may seem strange, but it is taken from real life.

An older woman, who was still the active head of an institution, died without warning one night in her sleep. The day before she died, she had a dream. She saw herself dressed as a bride approaching the door of a church, followed by various people on her staff. There was a bridegroom unlike anyone she knew, with somewhat the air of a symbolic figure. In her dream she had a great antipathy to the marriage and wanted to escape. This is a clear example of a point of view which inspires our dreams. The dreamer has seen her own death as a marriage, as a union with something new and strange, with the world on the other side of the frontier. Being reluctant to leave the familiar world of earth, she feared, in spite of the bridal dignity, that towards which she was going. Yet how true a picture of death, seen from the spiritual side, is painted in this dream, truer by far than waking thoughts could have made it.

When we want to understand the life of sleep and imagine what takes place there, even though it is hidden in oblivion, it is good to start by realizing how we leave our self-interest behind and become part of the world when we cross the frontier. What we can notice in our dreams is only a gentle hint of this great change in point of view. For this reason it is wise to prepare for sleep by putting aside willingly the self-interest of the day. By self-interest in this sense I do not mean something which is selfish or morally wrong. The state of self-awareness in which we live by day is the opportunity for self responsibility and self-sacrifice as much as for selfishness. It takes an effort of will for most people to put down deliberately the concerns of the day and leave them aside like the clothes we take off on going to bed. Strong emotions — either joyful of sad — can keep us awake. Both joy and sorrow belong to the daytime, and when they grow too strong, they bind the soul to earth existence, when it should be free. It is important to be able to take the events and cares of the day and disentangle one's feelings and attention from them before going to sleep. Then the mind should turn to the interests of the night and realize their great significance. This needs time and care. It need not take a long time, but there is great value in consciously placing an interval between day and night, waking and sleeping. Those who are busy until their eyes close of themselves, who , drop exhausted into bed straight from the rush of the day miss the opportunities for the inner life which are brought by sleep.

The most fruitful mood for this interval between day and night is thankfulness. In the next chapter we will turn to the exercise of looking back over the day, which we can do at this moment. Many people will find other things which they like to do at this time, for instance to read a page or two of a serious book. Whatever it is, a mood of thankfulness should be awakened in the soul. The anxiety, which so often clouds most of the daytime, should be laid aside. Can we really make our moods by our own will? If we do not try to do this, we are living entirely at the mercy of what comes from outside. What are we like then? In Thor Heyerdahl's description of the *Kon-Tiki* expedition across the Pacific Ocean on a raft, he gives an account of the daily behaviour of sharks. They are slaves to their emotions, which are called forth by outside circumstances. Calm creatures in a calm sea, they instantly get savage at the smell of blood. When I now say to myself, as I often do, don't be a shark, I am not thinking of myself as a profiteer but as a creature of moods and emotions. Sharks cannot change theirs but human souls can. Though it certainly costs a struggle, valuable moods and feelings can be created from within the heart.

Thankfulness is the state of soul that most readily allows the approach of spiritual beings. Angels are kept at a distance by clouds of fear and anxiety. We ourselves are imprisoned in our misery and cannot sense their presence. In sleep we shall be entering their world and during the time when we draw near to the frontier, they may come to meet us, even while we are still awake. It will not help to say: I have so many good reasons for being depressed and anxious. The other point of view is more fruitful which says: in spite of my anxieties, I would like to meet the angels and archangels; what is there for which I can be thankful, so that they may come near me?

Another reason for the importance of thankfulness is that thereby the souls of those who have died, to whom we had a particular connection on the earth, can approach our hearts. Like the angels and the company of heaven, we meet them on going into sleep. This does not mean that we are not connected with the hierarchies and the souls of the dead while we are awake, but the face to face encounter with them takes place in the world beyond the frontier. It is possible to seek out in thought a dead friend in the interval before sleep and to prepare a question to ask them. If the question is put rightly, the answer will often be found in the moment of waking. Some people find a contact with friends who have died, or hear answers to their questions in dreams. But the most immediate touch of the friend's presence is to be felt during the process of waking up. We all have friends and relatives around us on earth who influence our lives, but in sleep we find the host of those whom we do not meet in the body but who share in our human history far more intensely than we usually recall.

This interval is of value for another kind of asking. Most of us nowadays know what it is like to be bothered with problems that are very difficult to solve. We would like to see them in the light of a wisdom far greater than our own. We would like to ask questions of the beings in the spiritual world. This can in fact be done. Christ himself in our time walks beside us along the hard and perplexing road of life and will guide and help us in our decisions. Such questioning is best done before sleep. The answer may be there on waking, or it may appear in the course of the day, or even many days later. It is not easy to find the best way of putting questions and problems, so that they can be lifted into the clear light of the spirit. Any kind of self-seeking fear or anger darkens and blurs the question. Impatience confuses the answer. It can be especially valuable to form the question in the interval at the end of the day, if one has succeeded in filling this period with tranquillity and thankfulness. There is no need to have any doubts about whether one is capable of such spiritual conversation. The technique of asking and listening may at first be faulty, but this improves with practice. The matter is as practical as this, though the way of putting it is crude: if I want to speak French, I need to start, however stumbling my attempts may be; if I wish to talk with angels, I can do so, if I start to speaking. The courage to start brings the power to become more proficient in speaking. The greatest encouragement and joy can come from finding that such a conversation can succeed. Then the loneliness of our earthly existence ceases for a flash of time and we know from our experience that we are not left comfortless.

There are three particular ways in which we can find world-interest in the life of sleep. The fruit of these experiences of the night shows itself by day in the activity of our conscience. We receive in sleep spiritual substance for the conscience whose voice we hear when we are awake. The first of the three ways is as follows: On going to sleep we leave our personality behind. Our soul, in company with the self, goes out to meet other human souls. The soul lives at night in company with others, not just with those we meet in daytime, but particularly with those from whom we are then apart. The souls meet without the barriers of earthly circumstances. They come together in a form of universal democracy, without distinctions of class or race. We experience in the night that all human souls belong to the brotherhood of humankind. We meet other individual souls face to face without the trappings of daytime. The conscience of our waking hours is fed with this democratic interest in all our fellow-men and with concern for the individuals whom it will be our destiny to encounter again by day.

The interval before going to sleep is as much the time for praying as for asking questions. The thoughts we wish to send out to other people, the prayers we wish to offer for them, can be put at this time. They will be carried to meet the souls whom we seek in the world of sleep. An old tradition says that we should not go to sleep in anger with another person. Perhaps it would be better to say that it is good to wrestle with one's thoughts about other people so that destructive ones should as far as possible not be taken into sleep. Of course prayers and thoughts for others need not always be saved up until night. Whenever they are said and thought they will pass over in sleep into the world where souls meet. It is possible, though it takes a long time and is not easily done, to change one's relationship to another person by the thoughts that are directed towards him or her at night. If there has been anger and quarrelling by day, if the natural resentment can die down, thoughts of peace may altogether change the inner situation.

The second of the three experiences of sleep is that of meeting the souls of nations other than one's own. By day we are citizens of one nation, with our mother-tongue and home-land. By night we become international in the most universal sense. When nations are in conflict with one another by day, the souls of those belonging to them are especially attracted to each other in sleep. In this manner the social conscience of our waking hours is constantly cultivated and nourished. Our sense of taking part in the history of all humankind on earth is renewed each night. By day we often feel helpless in that part of our conscience, by which we share in the responsibility for national affairs and world events. What can I, one small individual, do about it all? At night we are outside our own skin and in the sphere where the souls of nations gather together. The thoughts and longings we take with us then show their significance. There are those human souls who are able in sleep to talk with archangels.

Just as our prayers for others rise into the world which we enter in sleep, so do those we offer for the nations and for humanity. This does not mean that it is wise to pray for definite political events. Anyone who puts imaginatively before themselves the thought that their prayers are directed to archangels will hesitate to speak and think in such terms. They may never have outer proof that their prayers have been heard. But they can be sure that all those whose thoughts are such that they reach the sphere of the archangels, are helping that the world-purposes of these spiritual leaders of humanity become stronger to prevail.

The third meeting in sleep is with the cosmos, with the stars and the beings who dwell in them. We owe so much in life to the heavens and what reaches us on earth from their influences. But we tend to take this part of life for granted. The sun shines down on us, the clouds send rain, the stars and the moon gleam in the darkness and we assume that this is all as it should be. The beings of planets and stars weave and work in our bodies and souls and we hardly notice that this is not just our own achievement. Nevertheless, when we go to sleep, the cosmos that we have overlooked or thought about in theory by day, becomes overwhelmingly real and significant. Somewhere in the depths of our daytime conscience, hidden and undeveloped, there is a sense that we have a measure of human responsibility in the cosmos.

When a human being becomes so advanced that they are an initiate and spiritual leader, they have to carry in their heart a very much more lively sense of responsibility than that of other people. For the initiate the word 'humankind' is no longer a vague generalization. They have to bear the weight of a sense of man's cosmic responsibility, of which other people scarcely even dream. Yet every night we divine something of this and take back to earth a need of it in our hearts. The seed may show itself in ways that are hard to recognize at first sight. A growing enthusiasm for compost heaps in the garden, an interest in the influence in the signs of the zodiac, the care for the natural environment — all of this points to this part of our conscience that is still buried.

Can our imagination extend far enough to pray for the earth and for humankind? Perhaps in our own words and thoughts we shall not be able to do so. But there is a prayer ready for us to use, so complete in its expression of man's des-

tiny on earth, that in saying it we are praying in this sense. It is
the Lord's Prayer. Familiarity and misuse may have made it
difficult for some people, but the imagination can take hold of
it again, when it is said as a prayer for man and for the earth.
At least it is worth pondering over the petitions again from
this point of view. It is one way to give expression in the waking hours to that which we have known while we were asleep.
By day we are very much confined within our own personalities but at night our souls are renewed and strengthened in
interest in other people, in the nations of the world beyond
our own, and in the kingdom of the stars. Through this we
gain a social conscience, an international conscience and a
cosmic conscience alongside our natural and necessary self-
interest.

Great as are our experiences in sleep, they also include dan-
gers. The two tempters of the soul, Lucifer and Ahriman,
approach us while we are away from the body. They are anxious to suggest impulses and feelings to us which will appear in
our minds by day as instinctive assumptions, as presupposi-
tions that we have not thought out for ourselves. It often happens that, waking up in the morning, we find our minds
clearer, new points of view present. Nevertheless, it is never
wise to take morning thoughts without giving them consideration and testing them by judgment. The wisdom of sleep can
be twisted and falsified by the tempters before we have had the
chance to test it for ourselves. It is good to watch and pray over
the moments of going to sleep and waking up again so that the
tempters may not spoil these times when the soul is especially
open to the spirit.

For yet another reason it is good to have a special short
prayer for falling asleep and waking up. The aura round the
earth has been filled with the direct presence of Christ since he
united himself with the life of the earth at his resurrection. In
sleep our souls pass out into the universe beyond this aura. In
the process of waking up they pass through it again on their
way back to the body. They stand for a moment in his presence

face to face. We are not yet able to know this with wakeful minds, but if the thought of this meeting comes daily into our minds, we are slowly prepared to wake up inwardly to it later on, while outwardly we seem to be asleep. It is most important that human souls should in time know consciously that they have passed through this presence on the return of the soul to earth. One of the best ways of preparing for this meeting is to choose a short prayer for sleeping and waking. There is a wide choice among old prayers, sentences from the Gospels and from the verses given by Rudolf Steiner. The following verses are by Rudolf Steiner.

Evening

There soars forth
From the depths of the world
The Sun of Christ.
Its light is Spirit,
It shines in the All,
It is Spirit in me
It lives in mine I.

Morning

It lives in mine I,
It is Spirit in me,
It shines in the All,
It is the Spirit-light,
It is the Sun of Christ
Which from the depths of the world
Comes soaring forth.

To some of those reading this chapter such a concentrated picture of our life in sleep may seem somewhat overwhelming. Naturally, such thoughts need reading over several times and much pondering to make them one's own. *No one should feel that they must think of all these aspects each evening before going to sleep, but the important point is to realize the contrast between the*

experience of our day-mind and that of our night-mind. First one and
then another element of the whole picture will become vivid
in our thoughts from day to day. As human beings we all lead a
double life and the more we are aware of this, the more natural
it becomes to be conscious of the change-over from day to
night and night to day. Some people may have to make the
interval before falling asleep and after waking up very short.
They may not be able to undertake much in this time. Yet the
very fact of being aware that a frontier is crossed, that the mind
is turning from self-interest to world-interest and back again
to self-interest awakens in the heart a greater sense for the spiritual nature of man.

3

The Life of the Day

In this chapter we will turn to opportunities for the inner life that meet us in the course of daily, waking life. They are, as a matter of course, of two kinds, those we make for ourselves deliberately through prayer and meditation and those that arise out of daily experience. At first sight, one might imagine that only what we do consciously affords us opportunities for spiritual growth. But though the distinction between two kinds of activity is real enough, both bring opportunities for spiritual experience. There can be a kind of give and take between the two aspects to our life in which each helps the progress of the other.

It is wise to try and arrange one's way of living so that regular times are set aside for inner activity. The periods need not be long but they should be undisturbed and free from other claims. This is equally true of private prayer and meditation and of common prayer, such as the Act of Consecration of Man, other church services or other events of communal spiritual activity. In earlier times meditations and services were, from a modern point of view, very long. Church services would often last all day. The Act of Consecration of Man, a modern form of Christian ritual, lasts less than an hour. It is not necessary to conclude that people today are less spiritually minded. It is rather the case that a different sort of concentration is required, which is usually best achieved for quite short periods. The most important point is not length of time, but intensity of attention. How to be wholly given over to spiritual activity, even for a few minutes, is the problem. Modern people, at least in the West, are restless of mind. Instead of controlling our thoughts, we are often pursued by them, like people worried by gnats or clouds of insects. The active inner life means hard work. This is brought home to everyone who tries to concentrate his mind intensively at will.

Some people grow discouraged by this kind of difficulty, even to the point of giving up all attempts to lead an active inner life. Others do not quite realize for a time how intensely their attention should be concentrated. A dreamy mood of warm, religious feeling is not sufficiently active for true prayer, meditation or partaking in a service. The fact of the matter is that nowadays the length of time required for the inner life is not really what hinders us. We are almost all of us living hurried, overcrowded lives, but a little care and planning can nearly always make free the short periods that are necessary. A quarter of an hour, ten minutes, will be enough. The real, effective hindrance is the intensity of attention needed for this short time. It is important to accept the thought, that real hard work can be done within the soul as much as outside in the world. There is a very common prejudice that work must be something that makes a noise and shows a visible result. The old Puritan grandmother of my childhood was pleased with those who knitted or baked, but disapproved of anyone who merely read or even thought. All the world's outer work, including the daily chores, requires effort, but the spiritual activities of the soul require it too. When we turn to the subject of meditation, we will return to this problem of intensity in greater detail.

Once one has accepted the fact that the inner life means effort and that our efforts at single-minded attention do not succeed easily, it becomes easier to work with it. The most important thing is not to give up because of discouragement or lack of success. Many activities in life require continual persistence and effort, for instance, learning to play the piano, or to speak a foreign language. Practice is necessary to achieve any skill. Most kinds of sport demand frequent exercises before they can be done well. It is no different in the inner life and it is just as natural that here too we have to go on practicing and trying for a long while without impatience. There is only one answer to difficulties of this kind and that is just not to give up, but to go on and on. Rudolf Steiner was once asked how someone could become a public speaker and he replied: 'If you make a fool of yourself forty-nine times, you will succeed on the fiftieth.' For some problems there is no cure but going on in spite of everything. This is especially true of the inner life.

Just because of this, a planned daily life can be a great support to our inner activity. A little time set aside at regular intervals means repeated efforts and the effort is spiritually more important than what is achieved. Time can help in two ways. A constant rhythm which is carefully kept can give force to our efforts. Routine is something rather boring and deadly. Rhythm, on the other hand, is alive and essential to the process of growth. This can be experienced quite simply in outer affairs. When a swimmer makes a stroke with arms and legs or a rower pulls at his oars, he must carefully time the following stroke or pull. If he makes his effort too soon, he stops what he has already achieved. If he begins again too late he loses all that was left from his previous stroke or pull and must start again. If his timing is good, the rhythm of his efforts gives him the greatest speed and progress. So it is also with inner activity. Rhythmic timing helps more than the amount of time spent.

In a second way, time comes to our assistance. The hours of the day have such a different quality. The clock is divided into twelve equal sections, but in our human experience they are distinct from each other. Early morning, midday, afternoon and evening have their own particular moods. Our souls do not pass through the hours in a straight line, but along a curve which at first leads downwards away from the worlds of spirit, where they have been in sleep, down into the sphere of the earth and then rising again in an upward curve. The deepest point of incarnation is not really midday, but a little later, round about five o'clock. The behaviour of small babies shows

this line clearly and their liveliest period is usually round about
this hour. Some times of day are better suited to inner activity
than others. Different people will have their own predilections
according to their character and circumstances, but quite apart
from this, there are certain impersonal considerations.
Midnight is, for instance, not a helpful hour for meditation,
nor on the whole is midday. Morning and evening, just after
and before sleep are good. It is of great benefit to make a short
space of a few minutes free after the midday meal in the early
afternoon. The soul needs to renew the connection with the
spirit in the midst of the day's stress, that the link may not
become too weak. The hours of the day are to be observed also
in common prayer. The Act of Consecration of Man is cele-
brated before midday, while the sun's forces are still rising to
their climax. What happens at the altar is thereby linked with
the great rhythms of the universe.

The times set aside for inner activity should be devoted to it
entirely. When they are finished, a clear transition should be
made to outer activity. This is the only way in which the two
can help each other. It is not useful to occupy some of the time
set aside for inner activity in thinking out daily problems. It is
often tempting to do so, because they present themselves so
clearly in such quiet moments. But if one resolutely concentrates on spiritual thought at such times, the clarity of vision
for the outer life will come later. It will certainly not be missed.
Neither is it useful to take over the mood of spiritual devotion
into the rest of the day. This only leads to unhealthy moods
and to disinclination for the duties of ordinary life, which are
due for respect in their own time. Anyone who has an active
inner life in a satisfactory rhythm, finds themselves controlling
and managing their space of daytime existence. They no longer
bob up and down on the world's sea like a cork on the waves,
pushed to and fro by the wind of events. They sail over the sea
like a ship of which they are setting the course themselves.
They become the managing director of their own life, or, a
much better picture, the creative artist working out his idea in

the material of daily affairs. It is good to think that we shape
our ends ourselves in matters of destiny, partly, at least. It can
be just as inspiring, though it is every bit as hard to achieve, to
think that we can shape and control the life of each hour of the
day, working with circumstances but not being mastered by
them. A wise explorer wrote once that he had never been seriously threatened on his journeys through the jungle by tigers
or snakes, but he had been nearly finished off by insects. It
seems more heroic to face tigers, but in fact we need the
courage every day to survive the insects. Anyone who leads an
ordered inner life will find that courage of this kind is greatly
helped by it.

Inner activity can be regarded as having three aspects for
which the terms may be used, contemplation, concentration
and meditation, in which prayer is included. Later on, the distinction between them will be described in detail. Each of
these three kinds of activity is something deliberately undertaken which requires effort and hard work. This point is
stressed here, because the most common danger for everyone
who wants to practice them is to follow the trend of their emotional reactions. That is to say, it is tempting to believe that a
meditation is more effective if one is in a good mood for it, that
a prayer is more intense if it comes out of a great longing to
pray. Such moods have their value, of course, but they are a
danger if the consequence is drawn: it is better only to meditate when I am in the right mood, it is better to pray when I
feel like it. It is quite easy to observe that people who take their
meals in this style get indigestion or become unhealthy. It is
just as true, though harder to observe, that the inner life can
become unhealthy in the same way. It is also dangerous to try
to estimate the results of a prayer or a church service by one's
feelings at the conclusion. The feelings are important, but they
should not determine one's judgment entirely. Feelings can
arise for so many different reasons and can be so misleading. I
once came across a lady, the mother of five children, keeping a
boarding house, who dashed along one day to the Act of

Consecration of Man for the first time. She dashed away in great dissatisfaction because, she said, she had not found peace. There are many far less obvious examples, which are really of the same kind.

The danger of emotional judgments in the inner life does not mean that it should become an affair of stern duty and grim effort. Everyone is aware of two layers of feeling in his soul, a surface layer of emotion and underneath a sphere of deeper, more lasting and less egotistical feeling. If one agrees with one-self not to take the surface emotion too seriously, the deeper feeling becomes more conscious. In this sphere there should be joy and enthusiasm for the inner life. There is joy in seeking the world of spirit, in opening heart and mind to the presence of Christ. The longing for this has first made us wish for an active inner life. Rudolf Steiner once said that there is nothing which the human heart desires so earnestly as to meet the spiritual world, and nothing which it fears so much. It is no wonder if the fear gets entangled with our emotions and makes them unreliable witnesses to true spiritual experience. Underneath, nevertheless, is the great longing and the deep joy, which can rouse the soul to the daily effort of inner activity.

The practice of the inner life at certain times during the day should not make us less active in or less concerned with the responsibilities of our outer affairs. On the contrary, it should have the effect of opening the mind's eye to see in the course of ordinary life how much spiritual experience is to be met with. It is not necessary to be always thinking of this, but it comes about quite naturally that those who practise inner activity are more awake and sensitive to the spiritual meaning of what is around them. Practical matters become more interesting and the ability to master them increases. Let us look at some of the ways in which outer activity can be spiritually fruitful.

The world around us is sleeping spirit. Everything that belongs to material existence has a spiritual origin. spiritual idea and force has incarnated into material forms and sub-stances. This sounds like an abstract statement, but it is in truth a living reality. The world has been created out of spiritual activity, which proceeds from really existing beings. They are not human and they do not walk about in bodies, but their energy and force is the source of what we see and handle around us. In the world of plants, insects and animals we observe easily that all living creatures are inspired and enlivened by invisible spiritual forces. In the world of things, however inanimate, spiritual forces are also present. There is actually no form without being around and with it. The world of matter is under a spell of sleep, so that we may imagine it to be dead. Yet it is not dead, but sleeping. In inanimate things the sleep is very deep, in living creatures it is light and dream-filled. Our human life is as we know it by virtue of the sleep of the spirit in matter. We move about in a comparatively still, quiet world, which we can take for granted and in which, therefore, we have the freedom to develop our activity.

What a difference it makes to the world around to be aware that it is not only the work of God, but that the divine beings still do not entirely leave it alone. There are nature beings living and weaving round all the creatures of the earth. Elemental beings are connected with the still unloving things. A walk down the street to catch a bus to work or to go shopping means contact with them. Their existence is affected by the way we meet them. It matters to the nature beings of the plants in the gardens or the park whether I look at them as I pass and whether I look with warm interest or coldly. Their whole development is helped by my interest and hindered by my lack of it, even if this comes only with preoccupation with other things. What a difference it makes to the daily jobs to realize that the beings belonging to things are affected by the way in which I sweep and dust, by the mood and attitude I bring to the chores. I can spread harmony or disharmony into the sphere of living beings by my own behaviour. There is nothing dull or boring about the material world, except when one looks at it materialistically. The true curse of materialism is that it makes people see a dull, flat, unprofitable world around them.

Another reason why the things and affairs of the material existence are significant for our spiritual life lies in the fact that we have come down to earth with a certain duty to experience and to learn to understand it. We should be busy gathering in the harvest of an earthly lifetime. When we come to the end of our time here, the fruits of experience will be taken with us through the gate of death into the divine world beyond. The divine beings, who helped once to create the world but now are somewhat withdrawn from it, wait to receive our harvest. What we shall have learnt on earth about the spiritual world will be a poor fragment to them. But they will be eager to hear from us about the realities and laws of the material world. They do not know such bodily experiences as the sensation which a human being has when he brings his two hands together and touches them. Neither do they know about mechanical apparatus, how different kinds of machines work, what can be done with tools. The spiritual beings hope to hear of these things from human souls, thus involving us in a kind of responsibility not to neglect our earthly opportunities. This thought can be worked out with a detailed application for which there is no space here. In general, it means that the affairs of the material world are of spiritual importance when they are experienced and understood in human minds.

In another sense outer life brings us into touch with the working of the spirit. We meet other people, they affect us. We ourselves speak and act. Events happen to and around us. In the weaving of destiny we meet spiritual forces and we handle them ourselves. The wakeful hours of our earthly life are our opportunity to work and to form destiny. During the time our souls spend in the world of spirit, whether in sleep or after death, we can have experiences, and we can be shaped and inspired by divine forces. But the time of our own activity is that which we spend in earthly consciousness. Here we can perform our deeds and work upon ourselves by facing the circumstances and facts of our destinies. We have to work with the spiritual forces of our own will. Nowadays earthly destiny seems to many people to have become a burden. Certainly great courage is needed to make 'a good job' of living in the world today. Nevertheless, the fundamental thought should never be lost that every hour of waking life is of inestimable value in our existence. Human beings have the opportunity of finding and developing their humanity in the 'great tribulation' of the earth, as it is called in the Book of Revelation. In sleep and after death they are moved by the will of God. Awake on earth they live in their own will and find the opportunity to grow more and more into the pattern of the human being, which is not yet attained in humankind. Human beings find the sense of their existence and the freedom to act in life on earth. Within the great design, in which man can become Man, even the burdens of existence can find their purpose, once one is convinced of the ultimate value of being alive on the earth.

The times of inner activity should be fruitful for the hours of outer work and destiny. Those people who turn to the spirit from time to time should be able to meet the responsibilities of earthly life with more vigour. In our work and destiny we have the task of incarnating something of the spirit into the world in which we live. This general statement, which sounds simple enough in itself, requires today a different application from what it had one or two generations ago. Each age in history has its special character which is formed not so much by the people who live in it as by the spiritual being who presides over it. There is a particular rank of beings in the divine world who are the guides of history and each takes a turn in watching over a period of historical time. Each of these has a special character and manner of working, which affects very deeply those human souls who are on earth under his regency. Michael is the name of the one who leads us today. In modern times he has reached a certain method of work which is new even in the course of his own development.

Today we are all of us affected by this influence when we try to act out of spiritual forces in our earthly destiny. We are unused to this new way, because it is different from that which

is familiar out of the past. In earlier times angels, archangels
and other divine beings would inspire human souls directly
with thoughts and intentions. They made their will known to
those on earth who were able to hear them. A classical example
is the inspiration of Joan of Arc. As a young girl, on a hot midday in her father's garden, she heard the voices that told her
what to do to save France. Perhaps no one of us today would
expect anything as clear and simple. Nevertheless, many are
apt to hope that we can in some way or another be told what to
do next. Today this does not happen; that is to say, not through
spiritual beings that serve Christ. No one should say today: the
spirit has told me to do this or that; or, this decision is wished
by the spiritual world. The Archangel Michael does not send
inspirations to people of what they should do. In the service of
Christ, he leaves human souls free, responsible for their own
thinking and doing. He waits for the freely offered activity of
human beings. This he takes up into his own sphere. He raises
it to something greater and more powerful than that which we
alone can bring forth.

This is a great change in history, a great development of
human responsibility. We may feel quite inadequate and long
for inspiration but the good gods will not give it to us. We have
to find our own ideas, our own will, our own decisions.
Nevertheless, what we think and do can be offered to Michael
and to Christ and they wait to weave our offerings into world-
evolution. Not only for ourselves, but for the spiritual world
also the doings and activities of our earthly life are full of
meaning. Those who practise inner activity will become those
whose outer activity can best become an offering to the being
of Christ. Great courage is needed to accept this new era of
human responsibility. But the time has come when the experience of true freedom can begin and this inevitably means that
each individual must be responsible for his own decisions and
actions. In prayer and meditation we call on the divine companions who are waiting for what we bring.

4

Looking Back on the Day

One of the many good results of looking at the daily round from the point of view of the inner life we consciously cultivate is that one can then begin to develop a certain mastery over the life of the day. How easy it is to feel, when the time comes to go to sleep, that the hours have passed in a vain effort to catch up with them, that nothing has been achieved or well done. How can one prevent interruptions and distractions from spoiling the day? The answer to all problems of this kind really lies in an inner attitude that gives mastery over the events. Naturally one has to meet the daily duties willingly as they arise. As a matter of course one has intentions for each part of the day as far as one is able to dispose freely of one's time and energy. But these duties and plans have to be woven harmoniously into the stream of time and into the flow of events. Some people let themselves be put off by everything that comes along. They often develop a wonderful good temper in face of interruptions and requests to do things unexpectedly for others. Nevertheless they are apt to be unable to end a telephone call or a conversation until long after it should have been finished. Other people are determined to achieve what they have planned, whatever the odds, however exhausted they get in the process, however much those around want peace and quiet. Somewhere between these two extremes there is another way. Like a skilful sailor, steering a boat through winds and currents, one can hold a course through the day, allowing for what comes from outside, but upholding nevertheless the purposes one has rightly undertaken.

In order to develop a certain skill in the mastery over time and events, so that time is not wasted and yet one has always time to use, it is necessary to cultivate an inner distance from events. One must be able to get outside the situation and look at it clearly from another angle. There is an exercise that can be done from time to time, or, best of all, each evening before sleep, to this end. It consists in looking back over the events of the day, from outside, so that one sees oneself as another person, and from end to beginning, so that one scene follows another backwards. Both these elements are important. As far as possible, one should make pictures in one's mind of the day's happenings. One should see them over again, but not through one's own eyes. One should picture oneself as an actor in the scenes alongside the other people. It is not easy to picture oneself walking into a room as one sees another person doing it from outside, to hear one's voice, watch one's gestures. It requires considerable effort to observe one's own part in an event, without readjustment or too much emotion. If anyone can do this, even to a small degree, they find inner freedom to get outside events for a few moments and see them from the distance with a new calm.

The effort which is to be made here is that of seeing from the opposite side. It is not necessary to make judgments or reproach oneself with weaknesses. That only obscures the value of the exercise. Yet experience shows that those who catch a glimpse of their lives from the opposite side in this way become more awake to the moral implications of what is said and done. The moral sense is roused more deeply than by much self-criticism. There is a story by Gerhardi which describes the weakness of looking at one's life to reproach oneself. It is about a man in Russia who acquires a long string of female dependants whom he never satisfies. They all come and reproach him, explaining the error of his ways. His reply is to point out that he has looked at himself deeply and knows that he is really far worse than they tell him. He reproaches himself much more than they do. There the matter ends. No

solution can be found to all these reproaches. On the other
hand, looking calmly at life from outside leaves the will free
to be roused. The soul is not exhausted by fear of short-
comings. It is encouraged by greater insight to a more active
concern with the problems of right and wrong that meet us
every day.

The other important effort is that of going backwards
through time. The exercise is directed towards developing 'the
other point of view.' This is done in space by looking at oneself
from outside instead of from inside. It is done in time by
thinking backwards through the course of the day. The true
meaning of such an attempt that may well seem like a kind of
mental gymnastics is only found by trying it out in practice. A
sense of well being and health of soul is soon to be felt when
the effort is made. The soul begins to experience a feeling of
freedom and refreshment. Instead of being confined to one
stream of time, the soul can expand into the fullness of time,
which includes a second stream. The one is part of our ordinary experience and flows from the past to the future. The
other is hidden from the sight of our minds by day, but in the
depths of the unconscious which we experience in sleep, the
stream of time from the future to the past is experienced. It is
difficult to imagine time moving backwards unless one has
lived with this exercise. In order to make this discovery it is
necessary not only to think over events from evening to morning, but to follow the *process* of the happenings backwards, even
as far as the movements that have been made. For example, a
walk down the street would be imagined starting from the
place to which one eventually came and moving back to the
doorstep from which one had set out at first.

Naturally, it takes practice to be able so to imagine events. It
is not necessary to go through all that has happened in the day
until one has acquired some skill. In view of the problem from
which we started, that of trying to have a mastery over the
course of one's day, it is better to set aside a short restricted
space of time for the exercise and do just as much as one can

then manage. More important than trying to cover all the happenings is the aspect of finding the other point of view in space and time. It may only be possible to imagine one scene, but this should be carefully pictured to show one's self from outside and one's movements going backwards. Walking down the street is a good example for experiment. To do this I should imagine seeing myself coming down the street towards me but moving backwards in the sense of arriving finally at the starting point of the walk.

How can such an exercise give inner health to the soul? Imagine yourself practising the exercise. All that you have done by the end of the day you see not yet done at the beginning. All that you have thought at the beginning of the day you see in the light of the experience you have gained by the evening. How much more thoroughly will one digest the happenings of the day by this method. The difference between what is important and unimportant grows clearer. One can better distinguish between the hindrances that one has really made for oneself and those that come from outside. One's estimate of what was well done and not so well done will change. The most valuable result of all can be summed up by saying that the experiences and events of the day will be well digested by this means. The unhealthiest element in the life of the soul is undigested experience and destiny. These consist of the things one is afraid to face, the responsibilities one would rather avoid, the experiences that raise big problems. Just as much there are ideals that one is eager to turn into deeds, efforts to help other people, work so well done that one can have a glimpse of how it can still be better done in the future. If all this is pushed away each night, un-thought out, or if it is seen again only as one has seen it in the bustle of the day, it becomes a burden in the soul. Undigested experience cramps the mind and constricts the heart with a sense of fear. The greatest fear comes from what one has not faced or will not see in one's life . Strength of heart and freedom of mind is the fruit of looking for 'the other point of view,' of finding the courage to get out of one's skin and see one's self from outside, to get out of the stream of time that flows towards what one is going to do into that which flows through what has been done.

Nothing is so much needed nowadays as a new source of moral energy and idealism. One of the greatest of modern temptations is to accept the standpoint that everything that one can get away with is 'all right.' Is it important to try to be truth-loving, honest in one's dealings, unselfish in one's way of living, devoted to high ideals? It is not easy to answer this question merely from the impulse of wanting to be a good person. It is certain that somewhere in his heart everyone wants to be a good person and yet never was there so much untruth, half-truth, quarter-truth, as there is today. Some of it is there in the name of good business, of success, of kindness towards the weaknesses of others, or just for the sake of not expecting too much of oneself in such hard times. How, in spite of all our weakness and the burden of present-day life, can ideals of goodness become more forceful? Not by reproach to oneself or others, but by vision. The kind of vision that inspires moral efforts can arise from this 'other point of view,' for it throws light on the deeper meaning of events and actions. The better experience is digested, the more clearly the moral values show themselves. Such vision is worth more than any amount of moralizing.

If the point of this exercise is not to make moral judgments and reproaches, in what mood should it be started? As far as possible the mind should be calm and detached, able to look back over the day from the distance in quietness. There is, however, no need to feel that one is facing life alone at this moment. Each human heart can find in Christ the immortal elder brother, who is the divine companion on the road of life. It is a great task to face one's destiny, even one day at a time. There is nothing strange in finding it too much for one's strength. Christ is always willing to help us in our helplessness. We can look for the light of his presence to shine upon our day and we can try to discover something of the vision which he gives to illuminate our view of life. We can ask for his strength to warm our hearts.

Anyone who tries, even if it is only as an experiment, to face their life or part of it in this way, finds themselves more able to get a certain mastery over the course of their day. This leads to the greater question of how to attain some mastery over the greater time-span of a whole lifetime. What happens from day to day is woven into the greater pattern of life, for which we may use the word 'destiny.' Do we endure destiny or do we shape it ourselves? This question leads to the further one of prayer. What can we rightly pray for, either for ourselves or for others? What should we ask of ourselves and what of God? Each person works out in the course of their life some kind of answer for themselves. It would be of no use to try to formulate a general answer that would hold good for everyone at all times. Nevertheless, there are certain universal facts about destiny which if they are understood lead to fruitful ways of answering such questions.

Each person has a pattern of destiny that belongs to uniquely to them. Another pattern is woven into this, that comes from the folk or nation into which they have been born, still another from the age of history in which they are living and a still greater one that works in their life because they are a human being, a member of humanity. Each one of us is the centre of a complex weaving of forces that bring events and experiences to meet us. How is this pattern controlled and directed? It is good to choose from time to time a short period of quiet in which to look back over some part of one's life. If this can be done without too much emotional distress, then the inner eye will observe a certain distinction. Some events can be clearly traced to certain doings and sayings of one's own. Even if there has been a time-lag between cause and effect, if the results were not what one intended, if one was not properly conscious at the time of what one was doing, nevertheless the effect of one's own behaviour is to be seen. Other events and experiences cannot be so explained. There is nothing within the memories of this lifetime, with the cause and effect discernible to one's own mind, to show why and how this or that should have happened. Is this the portion of destiny sent by God? The question as it stands is not quite true, for it implies another: How am I related to God?

I am not so related to him as if he were another person, wiser and more powerful than myself. He is the universal Godhead embracing all divine beings and with the divine part in me, I am also within God. The divine speaks in me in true thinking, loving feeling and in the voice of conscience. But I could never claim to know the whole of God with my small human self. Much of the universe of his divine being is beyond that which is in me. It is therefore a true experience that much comes to me from without my earthly self that is from the divine. The weaving of that part of my destiny for which I cannot find the immediate cause in my behaviour may be looked for in this sphere. But there is a further mystery. The whole of my true being is not contained within me as I know myself here on earth. One part of myself has remained behind at my birth in the divine worlds. It is my star that shines with divine light upon me, while I follow my ways on earth. This divinely nurtured self, that is more than I now am, weaves within the working of God into the forces that shape my destiny. What happens to me comes from God, and at the same time, without contradiction, is a message from my other self. God works in me; my self weaves in the working of God.

Comprehending this fact in all its implications takes a lifetime of experience. But to recognize it gives one a starting-point for the question of prayer. In the weaving of all destiny, I am myself involved, either in my immediate self here on earth or as my greater self that abides in the divine world. No hasty conclusions should be drawn from this fact, leading anyone to the attitude towards the troubles of other people, which says: In the last resort they have brought it on themselves, so it must be all right. The world-destiny of our time often takes a strong hold over individual destinies. Many people suffer much and

long for causes which are not rooted in their personal destiny.
Anyone today may be called upon to face suffering and loss for
reasons that go far beyond their own life. On the highest level,
though it may be hard to see, this is always for the sake of
bringing something to birth in the earthly world, that is not yet
there. The opportunity is always present in such suffering that
human freedom and divine love may increase in human life on
earth.

Starting from this point of view, how can we pray for help
in our lives and those of others? For we need to find that part
of our being from which true prayer can proceed. The divine
part within us can speak to the divine in the universe. The
impulse to pray may arise because we feel afraid, anxious, eager
to fulfil a wish, desirous to make someone else happy, to take
away their troubles. Such thoughts and feelings do not make
good prayers. Prayer is asking, but it is the kind of asking of
which Christ speaks in the Gospels: Ask in my name. This
means that the asking should be done out of the forces of
Christ in us. Our longings, wishes, thoughts for ourselves and
others have to be lifted up into the sphere of Christ and they
may change very much in the process. There is no selfishness,
even of the subtlest kind, in his presence. It may well be that
the mood that fills the heart as one tries to do this, is only that
of helplessness. I may feel: All that I can say about my own
destiny is that I don't know how to bear it; all that I can say
about another person is that I don't know how to help him.
The mood of helplessness has a quite special value and can
bring much good with it. The heart is then opened to feel
Christ and he can make his nearness known. Helplessness so
often arises when selfishness is laid aside and Christ can show
himself at that moment.

In the mood of true asking the thoughts are lifted up and
transformed. It will follow naturally that petitions requesting
something to happen or not to happen will not seem suitable.
It is unwise to pray for definite ends, even for the good health
of someone else. It is better to lift up one's thoughts of the

other person into the presence of the angels and Christ and to pray for their helping presence in the heart and the destiny of the other one or of oneself. Some people feel this most strongly if they use no words of prayer, but concentrate their strength upon gathering the thought of the other person. Others wish to use a form of words speaking to Christ or to God. Either method can be good, if the process of lifting up the thoughts and wishes is observed. The more we understand the being of Christ, the more real such prayer becomes. Asking is prayer, but not asking for something, but asking 'in my name.' We open ourselves and our friends to the power of the spirit that is greater than that which lives in us. We grow in spiritual grace, if we in our limitation ask the presence of that which is beyond us.

This kind of asking means the inner act of opening ourselves to the presence of the world of God. The result will not be that our destinies will be solved and arranged without our own effort. Prayerful asking rouses the awareness of the divine force in ourselves. It lifts thought and feeling to the forces of God in the worlds of spirit. Thereby the power of the Spirit can become more active in us and be at the same time united with the spirit of God. Our strength can be increased to work in our own destiny. We offer less hindrance to the working of God from without and find the courage to unite our efforts with it. We can come to accept what comes to meet us, so that it may be woven creatively into our further life. In this sense prayer can transform destinies. The divine answer will not be the removal of trial and trouble. It will be more likely to take the form of bringing a sense of creative purpose into depressing troubles or even into great overwhelming suffering. There is no senseless destiny if we can find the revelation of the divine in all that we meet.

In the previous chapter it was said that in the present age of Michael no one will hear from the good spiritual powers what they have to do next. We are, as human beings, asked to become responsible for our own decisions. Though this is so, it should not be understood to mean that spiritual beings are not interested in us and willing to help us. Christ himself, Michael — the guide of our time, the angels who watch over our individual lives, receive every thought and feeling of ours that turns to them. As we draw near to their presence our vision is changed, our ideals clarified and our courage to act on our own responsibility strengthened. Prayer means drawing near to the good beings of the world, whose nature is our inspiration. It does not mean asking them to do for us what we should do for ourselves, handing on the burdens that we should be carrying. It is a form of working together with the beings of God, who, through Christ, share in the destinies of man on earth. Co-operation with the divine powers is the fruit of prayerfulness. Walking in friendship with God is the prayerful life.

In the great red window that was designed by Rudolf Steiner to be placed at the door to the great hall in the Goetheanum there is, at the lower end, a small picture that stands by itself, though it is a detail of the whole. It represents the figure of a dragon with an astonishingly large eye in the head. Facing it is the figure of an angel with a sword pointed towards the dragon. But the angel is not looking at the sword or at the enemy. He is looking into the spheres of the heavens. It was Rudolf Steiner's custom to point out to those who saw this picture that the angel has strength to withstand the dragon because he is looking not at him but to the divine powers in the heavens. For us human beings prayer for ourselves and others is the act of looking, like this angel, to the divine powers. They will help those who seek them to stand firm in the midst of all that happens and to seek in the weaving of destinies the revelation of God's spirit.

Contemplation, Concentration, Prayer and Meditation

Turning now to the practice of inner life in times set apart for it, we find that it falls naturally into three parts. The distinction between them is not arbitrary, but inherent in the nature of things. Stress should be laid once more on the fact that nowadays each person is responsible to themselves for the conduct of their inner life, just as they are for their financial affairs or for the arrangement of their household. Rules that apply equally to everyone are not helpful. There is no intention of saying here that everyone must practise these three activities. That is for each person to decide and attempt for themselves. The angle from which the matter is approached here is the nature of the inner life in itself. The three parts are those which can be observed by everyone arising in the course of practice. They are naturally inherent in the inner life, as the three forms of thinking, feeling and will are natural to the life of the soul. It follows from this that the inner life is best kept well-balanced when something of each of these three elements is included. One-sided development and other forms of exaggeration would be avoided in this way. The desire for harmony is a good reason for deciding to aim at this threefoldness in one's inner activity.

Such a thought at once calls up the fear that besets almost all of us nowadays. How am I going to find time for so much? How am I going to adjust these aims to the claims of work, domestic affairs, and family responsibilities and to my natural wish to see my friends and to keep in touch with national and international affairs? What an undertaking it is to be a whole human being in these days, when we must be willing to do more and more things for ourselves. Is it possible even to try to be many-sided and of wide interests, as a human being is built to be?

One thought that gives a clue to this problem was discussed in the previous chapter. We have to find, as far as we can, a mastery over the course of our own life. It is important to discover something of the true value of time. The practice of a threefold activity need not take so much outer time, in terms of hours and minutes, if skill is acquired in entering thoroughly into whatever one is doing and then withdrawing as thoroughly from it. This applies to outer as much as inner things. The time consumed in a spiritual exercise is usually less than that spent in settling down to begin. It is therefore of great value for the inner life to become aware in all that we are doing, how much of our attention is engaged in the matter in hand. Of course, the manifold interruptions of modern life come to hinder our efforts. In the long run, however, hindrances tend to increase rather than weaken the strength of the power to control our interest and attention. If we can do something and then put it from us, whatever it may be and however unimportant in itself, this brings skill in the handling of time from a spiritual point of view.

Rudolf Steiner once gave some advice to teachers, which is very valuable in its implications for other problems. He said that there are economical and uneconomical ways of instructing children in things they should learn. For instance, they can, he said, be taught geometry so as to reach the Pythagorean theorem without strain in very much less time than that usually taken in schools. It is a problem of skill and economical handling of the material. This indication has a far wider application than teaching in the classroom!

Conversation with other people, for instance, can be economical or wasteful. Most true conversations, that are not just small talk, contain a moment when they come to fruition. The meeting with the other person has found its point and reason. It is not often fitting to end the conversation just at this climax. Mostly it is better to let it die away to a quiet close, which will not take very much longer. Should, however, the climax not be recognized by either of those who are talking together, the conversation may drag on long beyond its real conclusion.

In human relationships the same skill and economy can be found. The amount of time you actually spend with a person to whom you are bound by ties of affection or even of responsibility, matters less than the fact that you are present, that you can say or do something at the right moment. The implications of this thought go in all directions. What a change would be made in many a meeting, in sitting on committees and councils, in the writing of letters and reports, if it would be more generally recognized. It is an important clue to solving the problem of how to lead today a balanced human existence, including in a measure the practice of the spiritual life.

The three activities of the inner life may, for the sake of distinction and the convenience of a name, be called contemplation, concentration and meditation, which includes prayer. It is important to keep the distinction between them clear, so that they may not be confused in practise and lose their particular value. Contemplation, in this sense, is the gathering of spiritual ideas and the process of thinking them through, pondering them in the heart until they become living knowledge in one's mind. Concentration means the exercise of deliberately holding, by one's will, thought and feeling to one point for a certain length of time. Meditation is the third activity. The term is often applied in the common use of our language to the activity described here as contemplation. But something different is meant by meditation here. It means holding in the mind for a definite space of time spiritual thoughts and pictures, which are clothed in a concrete form of words, and concentrating all the inner energy upon this chosen content. The aim of the meditation, as that of prayer, is to open the soul to a meeting with the spiritual world.

Contemplation is the process of calling spiritual ideas into the mind and making them into the wisdom of life. It can start in a variety of ways. Books about the spiritual aspect of the world may be studied. Lectures may be heard. Groups of people may study certain subjects together. A sermon may be listened to, the Gospels may be read. From the depths of one's own soul thoughts may arise, which can become the content for contemplation. Some people find it a good plan to read passages from certain books each day in a quiet period, studying a very little at a time, one or two pages perhaps. This can be done in the morning by those who wake early and by others in the evening or the afternoon. What is read shortly before going to sleep quickly takes an independent life in the mind and can often be remembered vividly in the morning.

The material for contemplation can be gathered in many different ways, and at many different times. This activity does not depend altogether on regular time set apart. It requires only that the interest in spiritual things should be kept alive and be fed constantly. Contemplation may be practiced in two ways. The one is to keep the thoughts in mind during the day and in the time spent in sleep. It is not even necessary to be thinking about them continuously, but it is important not to put them away and quite forget them. We will then often experience that true spiritual ideas have their own vitality and growing power. They become more alive, they change, they put forth new shoots of further thought. They are transformed from something new and strange into the living substance of knowledge. This can happen by just keeping the ideas present in the heart from day to day. Experiences coming from outside will illuminate and confirm them.

As an example of what has just been described, let us take a passage from one of the Gospels, such as the scene of Christ walking on the water to meet the disciples in their boat on the lake. If one reads this passage or hears it read and then takes it into contemplation, the picture grows clearer and clearer in the course of the day's work and the night's sleep. Its meaning enlarges and different points of view keep emerging. Intellectual interpretations and problems fade and the deeper understanding of the heart awakens. One might think of the water as a picture for the vast, moving sphere of the life-forces into which the soul passes in sleep, when the dry land of the earth is left behind. Or, one may say, the water is the picture for the soul-life, where waves of passionate feeling, of wishes and fears, raise storms. The boat represents my self, tossed up and down in the gale, which it cannot control. Or again, one may imagine the sea to be the destiny of this world, through the storms of which I have to ride with my small destiny as if I were in a little boat. Looking from each of these points of view one sees, each time from a different aspect, the figure of Christ walking upright over the water, calming the storm, and one hears him speak, 'It is I, do not be afraid!' In this and in many another form, the scene may appear before the mind, becoming living experience from day to day.

The other method of contemplation needs time set apart definitely for reading and study. When an hour or two can be spared for serious reading, it matters very much how this is done. Experience shows that the books of Rudolf Steiner have a more intensive effect on those who study them than many others. Nevertheless, there certainly are also others to which that applies, which now follows. Let us consider the manner of reading. Very frequently a reader will notice a passage which particularly interests him or touches upon one of his problems. There is always a tendency to remember such parts more easily than others. This is not, however, the best point of view from which to read a passage from one of Rudolf Steiner's books. What he said and wrote was always composed with exact care for the process of thought running through a whole chapter or lecture. There is a path of experience through each

one, which influences the mind and changes the consciousness, if the way is trodden faithfully step by step. This can be
done by contemplating each thought as it arises, regardless of
its appeal to one's own feelings. A certain attention for the way
the thoughts follow each other is required, along with an eye
for the logic of the whole passage. By this means reading can
become an inner experience so strong that at the end on feels
as if one had passed through a great adventure or been on a
journey into another country. One can look back and say:
Something in me is different at the finish from what it was at
the start.

   A useful exercise can be practiced to help the development
of this kind of reading. Take one of Rudolf Steiner's lectures,
for instance, one from any of the cycles on the Gospels, and,
having read it, go through the thoughts again from the end to
the beginning. The path of experience will become even
clearer this way round. It is a good piece of mind training to
try also to remember the thoughts and pictures backwards
after reading a passage, without having recourse to the book
again. Such efforts greatly develop the power of true contemplation.

Concentration means gathering together inwardly the forces
of thinking and feeling by one's own will. It is the process of
getting hold of the soul forces and having them in one's own
control. The exercises by which Rudolf Steiner suggested that
this could be done produce a new kind of self-discipline. The
effort they require is that of the will, turned inwards upon
oneself. We are more accustomed to turn our will-energy outwards, in order to move and get things done. This is also necessary, but it can happen that the will is too often turned
outwards so that it collides with other people, or with circumstances, and too little inwards upon one's own heart and mind.
These exercises mean in the first place an effort of will but
they bear fruit in a new state of mind. In place of the confusion
of mind and hesitancy of aim and intention, from which we all

tend to suffer, they should produce order and clearness of sight.

There are five exercises suggested by Rudolf Steiner, which may be practiced so that once each day for a month one is done, and in the sixth month all five are included; that is to say each day a different one of the five.

The first is *concentration* upon an object for five minutes. A short period of time has to be made free only for thinking about an object quite unimportant in itself. It is good to have the thing in front of one's eyes. Anything will do: a window, a flower, a pin, a hand or a foot, a loaf of bread, or any other thing. The aim of the exercise is to keep the thoughts circling round the object to the exclusion of all else. A variety of thoughts about the thing are possible, but they should be directed again and again on to the chosen point. The *content* of the thoughts, whether one is well-informed about the object or not, is much less important than the *concentration* of attention. It is very valuable to practise the ability to direct the power of thinking at will. Obviously it is harder to do this with an uninteresting object than with an attractive one. As it is better not to attempt too much at first, it is often good to start with naturally interesting objects, such as a flower or animal, and come gradually to duller things. Nevertheless, after a time one comes to feel that nothing is dull.

The second exercise is directed to *actions.* It consists in resolving to carry out a certain action each day at the same time without omission. It is quite insignificant what action this may be. Actions which are necessary as a matter of course, like washing or eating, should not be included. The more trivial and unnecessary the action, the greater will be the effort to remember, and perform it. One can, for instance, decide to move something like a book or a vase from one shelf to another and then move it back the next day. This is not a waste of time and energy, because the aim of the exercise is not to do something useful in the world, but to change my own nature. Instead of swimming with the stream of necessities, I begin to think of controlling my movements and activities deliberately.

The third exercise is *tranquillity*. This can be practised in the midst of ordinary affairs. It is just a matter of choosing one's opportunity during the day to try by one's own effort to spread a mood of active quiet through heart, limbs and head. This will mostly have to be done against all kinds of disturbing influences from outside. The aim is that one becomes the master of one's feelings, so that one can create a mood at will. This kind of tranquillity is not of the sleepy, easy-going kind but is active and wakeful. It comes from inner effort rather than from favourable circumstances.

The fourth exercise is that of *positivity*. By this is meant deliberately practising at a certain moment during the day the effort to see what is positive in the things and in the people around. One is not required to overlook what is faulty and depressing or to argue it away, but deliberately to look for something to admire, instead of allowing the critical faculty to have everything its own way. Walking down a dingy street, for instance, one can try to find something beautiful, however hard one may have to look: the sunlight bringing out the colour in a brick wall, a cloud sailing overhead, a drop of rain on the end of the umbrella spoke, or a child's face. To look deliberately for something positive means an effort of will to use feeling in a direction chosen by oneself.

The fifth exercise is that of *open-mindedness,* of abstaining from making judgments. Without even wishing it, we are constantly arriving at judgments about what we see and hear. We hear a piece of news and say: I can't believe it. Or someone expresses an opinion and we say: What rubbish, it is not like that at all. We read of something being done and say: That is all wrong, it can't work. Someone expresses a view like our own, and we think: That's right and good. The problem here is not whether our judgments are correct. The effort required is to stop oneself from exercising one's power of judgment and leave the mind to open itself in wonder to the world around.

Every judgment closes the mind a little and though in itself it may be good, something of a further, wider view may be obscured. Judgments must, of course, be made, but for short periods, chosen at one's will, a deliberate attempt can be made to discipline and control the power to make them in favour of the open mind.

Contemplation is the act of carrying spiritual ideas down into the soul. Concentration is the drawing inwards of the will to control the forces of the soul. Meditation and prayer are the lifting up of the soul to meet the world of God. Both the other activities help to make the heart and mind capable of this third one. Prayer and meditation require a definite space of time set aside regularly from every other interest and duty. It is not necessary that the time should be long. In fact, it is better to keep it short, but it should be quiet and uninterrupted. How these spaces of time can be fitted into the life of the day has already been mentioned in earlier letters. The question here is, what is the effort required in meditation?

A meditation requires a definite content. The same is true of prayer. When one is praying for another person, a wordless lifting of the heart to God in the thought of the one for whom the prayer is made, may be fruitful. But in other respects a content, carefully chosen, is necessary. To concentrate all the forces of the soul and to lift them up without definite words is like walking along a road with your eyes shut. You may come straight to the point you were aiming at, or you may swerve aside without knowing it or collide with obstacles, and do yourself harm. Just because the words are so important, they cannot be chosen for any reason of taste and liking. From what point of view then? The words, which carry the thoughts and pictures of a meditation, are the place where the human soul can meet with God, with the angels, archangels, and all the company of heaven, who are members of his being. Our human words and thoughts are too 'self-bound' to make a meeting-place. This is the natural drawback to extempore prayer. We need to put our thinking, feeling and will into words, thoughts and pictures, which are true in heaven as they are on earth. This is how a right content for meditation is to be sought.

Where can such be found? There have been people from time to time, who understood language from what we might call the angelic point of view as much as from the human. They could choose the thoughts and words in earthly language that make a true spiritual encounter possible. The evangelists were inspired with an understanding for this. The beginning of St John's Gospel is a most valuable meditation, as are the words spoken by Christ to describe himself, the seven 'I am's.' In modern times Rudolf Steiner understood language in this way and wrote a variety of verses for meditation. During his lifetime, he gave certain forms of words to individual people. These were kept as the private possession of those who received them. All the published verses are free for everyone and will always prove reliable. There are forms of prayer handed down from the past, which some people find valuable. They are sacred words, which can be good guides to the soul seeking connection with the spirit.

Is there than a distinction between prayer and meditation? Some people held that the difference is great and that there are two kinds of person, these who pray and those who meditate. Some even go so far as to regard those who pray as less advanced and those who meditate as more advanced. This is a view with which I cannot agree. Prayer and meditation seem to me like two aspects of the same activity. Prayer is the activity seen more from the point of view of the human soul, who seeks the spirit. Meditation is the activity seen from the point of view of the community of heavenly beings, who look for a meeting with the soul. In both, the activity will be the greater according to how energetically we direct the forces of think-ing, feeling and willing to the spirit. If our prayer seems to require less effort than meditation, it is because we are not praying so well.

This subject of the threefold activity of the inner life is too large for only one chapter, and will be continued. In conclusion just one thought should be added. We are capable of the activities of the inner life through the creative power which was planted into human souls by Christ himself. They are part of the 'Christ in us.' His resurrection bears fruit in us, when his creative power flows into activity. I can pray to Christ, but I pray in Christ. Our inner strivings are the fruits of his resurrection; when we make the resurrection real in our minds and our hearts, we are practising the inner life.

6

The Self and the Threefold Inner Life

In the previous chapter the attempt was made to form and express a clear conception of the three parts to the inner life, contemplation, concentration, prayer and meditation. Now, with this in mind, we can think over our own relationship to these three activities.

What part of ourselves is engaged in them? What happens to us, or could happen to us, through the efforts we make? It is the common custom of all normally developed people to go about saying 'I' of themselves — I hope, I want, I will, I do not like, I can't or I can. We could not count the number of times we use such expressions daily, without thinking or having to make a special effort. Indeed, if one tries deliberately in writing letters or in conversation not to use the word 'I,' then a great amount of effort is required. It is an interesting experience, if it comes one's way, to meet a child or an older person, whose development is retarded and who can speak, but has not discovered how to call himself 'I.' He may say 'you' to himself or use his name in the third person. Meeting such a person demonstrates clearly what it means to us that we are in present times capable, from about the age of three years, of saying 'I' in all its forms as part of our usual consciousness.

Nevertheless, the way in which we use the word 'I' varies very much. For the most part in ordinary life we use the expression without filling it with true substance. On special occasions, when we say something of great importance, well considered, we can say 'I will' with the force of our whole being. This distinction, which we can all experience, points to a deep cleft in ourselves. The form of the 'I,' that is to say, the consciousness with which to say the word, and its substance, are divided in us. They can come together; they do so whenever we use the word with true meaning and weight, but it is quite natural to us, as we are today, for them to be separated. It is no effort for us to say 'I' quite emptily or with only a small part of ourselves present. On the contrary, the effort is required when we do actually bring form and substance together and use the word with consciousness and weight.

This observation goes to show that our true self, the individuality which is the spark of the spirit in us, is not always present when we say 'I.' In fact, a different part of our nature is often making use of the form of the 'I.' This is our *personality,* through which the selfishness of our capacity for selfhood is usually expressed. Personality distinguishes each of us from the other. It is woven together from the disposition which we have brought with us into life, from the characteristics which we inherit from our families, from our surroundings, the kind of school we went to, the way we were brought up and the experiences which we have had.

When you meet another person it is much easier to see his personality than his true self. You can quickly see something of his background, circumstances and upbringing. If you are observant, you can perceive some of his qualities, his cast of mind and disposition. But you will not see much of his true self, unless you meet him in an extraordinary situation, when all the support of custom and environment is removed, in one of the testing times of life. Then you may be able to see this hidden self in a flash of insight. It is the same with ourselves. The familiar part of us is the personality to which we have grown accustomed in the course of years. A great upheaval of destiny, some kind of shock, may shake this acquired personality to pieces and a new one may gradually emerge. This is a painful process but very valuable in one sense, because through such experience one knows as a fact that the personality and the self are not the same. When the one is shattered, the hidden lasting strength of the other shows itself. At some moments in life, one feels, I can't continue any longer, I have lost the strength to go on living. Time passes and one is somehow or other still living, though from day to day one does not know how. The true self can endure, when the personality is incapable.

The true self is undeveloped, is scarcely born yet in most of us. The personality was born as we grew up and entered on the experiences of life. The self must be born again out of the spirit. Earthly conditions and the people round us have given us personality. Sometimes a leisure moment can be spent conjuring up memory pictures of some of the people who have influenced us and made us what we are. Our family has certainly played a large part in childhood, as did teachers during the school years. But there are usually many others; a neighbour, a friendly shopkeeper, another child or a hero to whom we looked up in awe. Rudolf Steiner suggested that autobiographies should be written expressing gratitude to all those to whom one owed character-forming experience. His own *Story of my Life* is a model of this method. Only by reading between the lines can one guess how hard was the struggle of his growing years, how much misunderstanding and loneliness he suffered. Yet all through the autobiography he describes what was valuable in all that he received from other people. One can thank the world around for assisting in the birth of the personality.

We owe the spiritual essence of the true self within us to Christ. He came to earth and went through Golgotha for the healing of humankind and gave to each human soul the seed of true, spiritual selfhood. Since that time each of us may go through the second birth out of the spirit from within. The process of this birth depends very much on whether we wish it to take place, or whether we cultivate consciousness of the spiritual element, of the new, still childlike being hidden within us. The personality develops through reflection from what is around, and is moonlike in character. The Christ-given self grows from within and sends its forces into the world around, for it is sunlike in its nature. But the second birth, that of the sun in us, will not happen without our will and our activity. The new man, the higher self, will grow and develop if we are willing to give it the opportunity.

The true self is the part of us that is active in the inner life, in contemplation, and concentration, in prayer and meditation. Some of us may have personalities which naturally incline to an interest in spiritual things. But the force of personality will not carry anyone far along the hard way of daily effort. The enduring activity of the inner life can only issue from the creative power of the true self. Every effort in this direction means calling upon the forces of this being. When this happens, opportunities are given for its development. An active inner life actually alters our nature and helps the process of the second birth to proceed continuously in the soul. Let us look for a moment at one of the reasons why the birth of the true self is so important at this time.

One of the most common difficulties that we all have with ourselves today is that we so easily have divided minds. One part of us wants one thing, but another part is working in quite another direction. We may suppose that the conscious part is the important and decisive one and then find ourselves behaving in a way that we were unprepared for according to our conscious intentions. How awkward it is, too, with other people who are like this, or, as we generally think, are much more so. One comes across many today who are capable of the greatest contradiction in behaviour, so that their friends do not know whether they are meeting the same person in the evening who was there in the morning. An extreme example of this problem was told to me by a friend from the former East Germany, who described a Russian officer at the frontier to the West. He picked up the traveller's passport and told him that he might cross to the West, but stamped a mark in it meaning that he was sent back to the East. This seemed to be a frequent occurrence, not because the officer made a mistake, which could be pointed out to him, but because his mouth was speaking with one part of his being, while his hand moved from another, whose intentions were different.

There is a widespread tendency, of which this example is only one, for the soul life to fall apart in people today. Everyone is threatened by the danger. These moments of unreasonable indecision, of divided mind, of contradictory behaviour, which we know so well, are only symptoms. Personality changes through life as new experiences are added to the old, as character is altered by events, by whether outer success comes along or failure, by whether ambitions are fulfilled or disappointed. The influence of what comes from outside in personality is very strong. Because, as human beings, we are capable of selfhood, we can be selfish and over interested in our own wishes and fears. The self-seeking of the lower self often expresses itself through personality. Nevertheless, we are aware that selfhood is the opportunity for self-control, self-responsibility, self-sacrifice. Another higher self, the spiritual being in us, is present and though this is different from and beyond the personality, it can from time to time overshadow it and change some part into its own image. The personality may often use the form of the 'I,' but the true self is expressed when form and substance speak together.

What is the soul? We use the term that can be used vaguely to describe our inner nature. We tend to take for granted that it is a unity, as did the dramatists in the later Middle Ages, who liked to put on the stage a single symbolic figure called Mansoul. In reality our human soul is not onefold but threefold. Its existence is the interplay between thinking, which we experience centred in the region of the head; feeling, which belongs to the heart, and will, of which we are most aware in our limbs. All these three activities make up the life of the soul and though they are so far connected with the body as to be held together in an appearance of unity, their forces are different and distinct. The unity may break down at any moment and this in fact often happens nowadays. The head thinks one thing, but the feeling may have other views and the willing may act on its own. Many difficulties come about because the unity cannot be maintained as a matter of course.

In the Rudolf Steiner's Mystery Plays, a picture is drawn of the healthy life of the soul. A human being is shown accompanied by three soul friends, Philia, Astrid and Luna by name. They describe their different tasks, the forces which belong to them and the help they can give to the human self. They group themselves around the one whom they are accompanying and give her strength and counsel. They show themselves as the spiritual counterpart of what we know in ourselves as thinking, feeling and will. They are in harmony with each other, but their unity comes from the higher self, of whom they are the companions. When we become aware of our true self and help its growth, we are finding the force of what makes for unity within. The self should become the true master within the soul.

When the unifying force of the self is active, it is not necessary for thinking, feeling and will to say the same. The human being can become integrated in a new, freer way. If, for instance, someone is insulted or badly treated, he can decide for himself what his feeling shall be, putting aside the natural reaction of being grieved. It may, however, be necessary to reply to the insult, and his thinking will think an answer in accordance with what has been said. At the same time some kind of action towards the one who has treated him badly may be required and his action may not be the logical consequence of his reply. He might, for instance, find it necessary to think and even speak from the logic of what has been unjustly said, but his action might be a kindly one. From the standpoint of another person, he might seem to be very much of divided mind, thinking, acting and feeling differently at the same time. This might be a sign of disintegration in the soul on his part, were he behaving out of his personality, but if the higher self is in control, his behaviour will be integrated. He will indeed be a little nearer to freedom, when he is not obliged to impose consistency on his thinking, feeling and willing and yet he is living as a whole human being.

Why do so many people today seem to their neighbours to be so unreliable? Why is everyone so afraid of responsibility? Why is it so difficult to face facts, that many people are to be found protecting themselves from reality by erecting their own scheme of things and denying everything that does not fit in with it? We are afraid of our own nature and of the world. Nevertheless, there is something on which we can rely in ourselves and which other people could trust in us. This is the higher self, who is born through the second birth. The less the personality blocks the way, the more the true self can act as master within the soul, the nearer we shall come to being 'whole' people. Responsibilities will not be taken lightly but the strength will be forthcoming to undertake them. The circumstances will not be easier but the source of active, sunlike courage will be found in the self. A new relation will also come about between the personality and the higher being. They will grow into harmony with one another, as the personality changes. It will cease to be entirely the reflection of what comes from outside and will take on the character of the true self hidden within the soul. Moonlike, it will still reflect the sun, but now it will be the sun within.

Let us look at one of the many ways in which we can see how the self is active in contemplation. How does someone read a book, who is not making the particular effort of contemplation? He looks for what interests him immediately and passes over the rest. Some people tend chiefly to read what they agree with in a book or an article. Others are stimulated by something they disagree with and look for the opportunity to 'think against' what someone else has written. Both are reading for what interests them personally. Of course we all read in this way and must do so, even from the point of view that many books do not deserve another method. It is a special art to find what is valuable in a book without looking on every page. Contemplation, however, is different. If we choose a book, a chapter or even a page of a book for contemplation, it will be something of which every sentence is worth being read. It is a useful experience to go through the same passage more than once. This involves overcoming the natural tendency of the present time to pass quickly from one thought to the next. Nowadays there is so much to be read that one is easily haunted by the sense of not being able to keep up with everything for which one would like to have attention. Why then read the same thing many times? Contemplation is different from wide reading and it is hardly possible to find the way of deepening one's thoughts without returning to what we know well again and again, whether in reading or in thought.

It requires a conscious effort of will to overcome these two natural tendencies: to notice only the ideas which immediately interest us; and to regard a thought once grasped as finished. Still another urge of the modern mind has to be surmounted in contemplation. We read in order to know more, to possess it like a kind of inner wealth. Contemplation enriches the heart and mind indeed, but not because it leads to remembering everything we have heard or read but by virtue of that which becomes part of the life within us. The fruit of contemplation should be the living substance of wisdom in the soul. That which has been taken in intellectually and then forgotten may nevertheless be part of this inner treasure. More important than being able to recall or explain the thoughts are the depth and intensity with which we have experienced them.

The activity of contemplation is not to be carried out by following our natural tendencies, but by overcoming them through a deliberate effort of will. In so doing we call upon the self, the higher being within, of whom in the best sense we say 'I.' The personality supplies, for instance, the natural attraction to certain ideas. If something has happened to me recently, and I read a passage that helps me to understand it better, I tend to be more interested in this than the rest of the book, whilst another person might be much more impressed by a different chapter. But if I am using the whole book for the purpose of contemplation, I shall need to rouse my interest deliberately for the whole and follow the thoughts in their own order and logic in spite of my particular interest in one. The power of the self can achieve this and in so calling upon it, I help to continue the process of the spiritual birth within me.

When the self is thus actively engaged in the inner life, it has the effect of making one feel inwardly freer than before. I can, for instance, face unexpected experiences more calmly. There may be nothing in my past or my upbringing to guide me in dealing with them but I can feel an inner strength of greater power than the confidence which custom gives. I shall find myself less easily overwhelmed by the turmoil of the emotions, because, as the self becomes more real to my consciousness, it will be more able to control this turmoil. A source of greater courage will become available to me and I shall find myself less restricted by fears.

Concentration can be a means of bringing the true self to birth as well as contemplation. Exercises of concentration involve doing something from within that requires a particular effort of will in the opposite direction to that which comes by force of circumstances and outer events. It is unimportant what object I choose. The important fact is that I have decided to concentrate my thoughts on one point, without any motive from outside, and I carry out my decision. When I choose a habit to cultivate each day, I am not doing something which I am obliged to do for outer reasons, like washing up or making the bed. I am performing an act, however small, which has no outer significance, so that my self may practise mastery over my actions. Tranquillity, positivity and open-mindedness are all attitudes of mind which I have to cultivate with conscious effort, because they are the opposite of the feelings to which I am most prone out of my natural reactions. Very few people are so untouched by worries and problems that they can be tranquil of heart without the effort to overcome anxiety. Very few are so satisfied with life that they can see the good in what is around without the effort to overcome negative criticism. Very few are so free from judgments that they do not require to make an effort to stop the process of forming them. Only our will used freely by our own decision can perform these exercises.

Meditation and prayer are essentially the activity of the true self. Much of the difficulty experienced by many people in their practice is just that of getting past the other parts of one's being which often speak in us when we use the word 'I' and penetrating to that part which is truly 'I' and which can go to meet the world of God. We are, for instance, accustomed today, when we take something seriously, to have many thoughts about it. We come first of all into an intellectual activity. This is not to be avoided but we should realize that this is not meditation but only a stage on the way to attaining to it. When words have been chosen for a prayer or meditation, it is natural that we first try to understand them. But then thoughts about the content should be put aside and one's strength directed towards entering into the thoughts, picturing them, hearing the words, deepening the feeling and inner sense for them. In this manner one passes beyond the intellectual reflection of the self into the depths where it is truly at work. We are so little accustomed to leaving the intellectual sphere behind, that practise and persistence are needed to reach the level of the real self. We should not be disheartened by the difficulty. In moments of discouragement or great weariness it may be good just to read over the chosen words again and again, listening to them quietly. In this way a beginning is made without strain.

One very good method of becoming more familiar with the true self is to study Rudolf Steiner's *Calendar of the Soul*. In a series of verses for each week of the year, the relation between the self, the soul and the world is described as it unfolds in harmony with the seasons. A rhythm which continues throughout the year in the depths of our human being is lifted into consciousness and thereby the life of the self becomes better known to us. If some passages seem hard to follow, they will become clearer if one starts to read them with the question: what happens to the self at this season? What happens in the world? The drama of the passage then begins to unfold itself.

In ancient times the second birth was the secret of certain chosen people in the temples. Since the coming of Christ it is a mystery which belongs to us all, for the fulfilment of which we can all strive. It is that for which we all long in the present age, whether we realize it or not. The dissatisfied soul of today yearns for the spiritual fulfilment, which is found through the true self, which Christ has brought to humankind. All the strivings of the inner life help us to find ourselves in this sense, and foster in us the spiritual process of the second birth.

7

Meditation and Prayer

The theme of the last chapter was the relation between the inner life and the birth of the true self. Those who practise contemplation, concentration, meditation and prayer find changes coming about in themselves that are to be understood only through the realization that the Christ-given self has only just begun the process of emerging within the soul. We need this self for the sake of meditation and at the same time the effort to practise it calls this part of our being into existence. One of the problems of the inner life lies just in the fact that we cannot practice any of its activities by following our nature simply as it is in ordinary life. We have always to change something in ourselves, in the way our minds work, before we can pray or meditate effectively. Nevertheless, the forces that we need are all present in us. The question that we have to ask is which forces should be called upon to develop and which should for the time being be set aside. It is, for instance, quite obvious that to concentrate we have to overcome the natural tendency of our attention to wander from one thing or thought that attracts us to the next. Our will, which naturally tends to be directed outside into what we say and do, is then drawn inwards and controls the stream of our thoughts. As long as the exercise lasts, our natural habits of mind are changed by our own free will.

What happens in the process of contemplation is likewise not difficult to observe. In the ordinary way we go about our affairs, forming thoughts and opinions about what interests us. We say: I think this and you think that. In contemplation we deliberately put aside the thoughts that we have naturally and allow the thoughts of the world to live in us. We begin to find a new kind of thought. It is not difficult in practice distinguishing between the two kinds of thinking. The one, which comes easily nowadays, is thinking *about* things from my own point of view. The other, which has to be cultivated deliberately, is allowing the world thoughts to *think in me*. Supposing, for instance, that someone visits an orchard, from which he hopes to have a crop of fruit. He can estimate its extent and think out the merits of the different kinds of applies and pears. He may think wisely about pruning and protection against pests. Quite another thinking begins, however, if he allows himself to contemplate a pear or apple tree for its own sake. Then the tree in its true nature, with its character, shape, style and gesture, begins to live as a thought in the mind of the thinker. He could say with reality, the tree thinks in me, a part of the world thinks itself in me. This kind of thinking is brought about by an act of will performed by the self.

In the matter of meditation and prayer the process is somewhat less easy to follow. When the attempt is made to think it through, some description of the following kind emerges. What is said here is only a bare and simple outline, not in any sense exhausting the subject, but it may be taken as an example of what each of us can and may do for himself in making the effort to think over the meaning of meditation. The beginning of a meditation is the attempt to shut out the impressions from the world around through the senses and to put aside all one's usual thoughts and feelings. Then the mind concentrates inwards upon itself and the will is drawn up into the thinking. The will is the means of directing the forces of thought and feeling upon the meditation. The content, that is to say, the words to be meditated upon, now occupy the mind entirely. The next effort will be to stop oneself thinking *about* the words and trying to find meanings for them. As long as this happens, our present earthbound self or personality is in charge, directing our intellectual thinking. Of course, as we have the gift of intelligence, we have to start by thinking about the words and their meaning. This is a stage to be accepted and then overcome. At this point the natural habits of the mind are deliberately changed. The process by which this can be done is to enter into the words, both in sound and in picture, as if one would penetrate through them. Words do not only convey meanings, though they are often handled in this manner. They can be so approached that they come to life, spread their wings and carry the soul towards the spheres of the spirit. That is the reason why words for meditation have to be chosen carefully from the writings of those who know the spiritual effect of language. The actual words in sound, in their relation to each other, in their meaning, are of great importance.

It is clear that the forces of the mind are called into activity in a different manner than they otherwise are in the course of daily life. The power of comprehension sinks into the background and other capacities are brought into the foreground. These are especially the ones that allow us to form inner pictures at will and to listen inwardly to sounds and rhythms. We all have the faculty of creating mental pictures, which we use constantly when recalling past events from memory. We actually create our own inner pictures when we bring back into remembrance experiences that we had once in the past, thoughts that we once thought, scenes that we have once witnessed. This capacity is called upon in the process of meditation, not in order to reproduce something that happened in the past, but for the sake of entering vividly into the experience of thoughts which are the content chosen for meditation. Some people are more aware of the ability to form inner pictures than others. Those who find it difficult to realize that they can do this may be greatly helped by contemplating a favourite painting, one of Raphael's or Michaelangelo's, for instance. It is possible to use a picture for meditation instead of a form of words, with, of course, the same condition, that it is painted by someone who knew how to represent spiritual realities truly.

To do so may be a valuable encouragement towards forming
one's own pictures.

The capacity of inner listening to sounds and rhythms is
also connected with the ability to recall sounds once heard. In
meditation it is not a question of remembering sounds; they
have to be born into existence out of the form of words that
make up the content. This means a process of inwardly speaking the sound and melody of the words as one is listening to
them. It is not necessary to be concerned with one's feelings
about the words or even in the first place about the meaning
that one attaches to them. Meditation has a way of giving rise
to feelings of a new kind and of bringing ways of understanding, which are not to be reached by only trying to grasp the
content. But this new feeling and understanding cannot come
about unless one has the confidence to start from the words as
such and let them become a living experience in sound,
rhythm, picture and thought. This whole process begins with a
kind of inner speaking, which is active listening at the same
time.

What is important in meditation is to call these capacities
into activity, to make efforts of this kind. The result is of less
significance than the efforts made. By making them we are
drawing near to the beings of the spiritual world. They can
come from the other side and fill out with their presence what
we have attempted to produce. The problem of meditation is
really this: how can we so use our capacities that the beings of
God can draw near, be with us and speak to us. Every attempt
at meditation is a request to the spirit of God to fill our hearts.
Here the question arises: Is it not then better to use forms of
prayer in which we directly address God or Christ? If we are
actually asking for the divine presence, why then use other
forms of words that may sound like statements? Such questions can be answered individually. Some people may well find
it better to pray in words that express a request for the presence
and help of God. Others may experience the lifting up of the
forces of heart and mind through the process of meditation as

a continual request for the indwelling of the spirit. Some may wish to remind themselves in words that they are drawing near to Christ. Others know without the words that in seeking the spirit, they seek him. Whichever way is chosen, it is true that Christ's presence is a spiritual reality and has to be sought by spiritual means. In a sense he is very near to us, since he has chosen the world of earth for his dwelling and is our constant companion through all the trials of human destiny on earth. Nevertheless, he is spirit and is to be sought in truly spiritual ways. It is not so important to repeat his name over and over again, as to know how to seek his immediate presence.

All that we do by our own efforts in meditation and prayer is only one half of what is happening. The touch of the spirit is the answer. The growing of spiritual reality within heart and mind is the fruit. The effort to be made in meditating may take up much of our attention, but the idea of the whole process should not therefore disappear from view. Meditation and prayer are conversation with the divine world and an essential part is the opening of the inner ear to hear what comes from the other side. The entire answer may not enter our consciousness all at once. Thoughts that have their origin in those moments may appear in the mind later, during the course of daily life. Nevertheless, the need for the open ear should not be overlooked during the process of meditation itself.

We have seen in the foregoing pages that the practice of the inner life requires the forces of the true self. They have to be called into activity for its sake. However, although this effort has to be made especially at the time when exercises are done, two habits of mind cultivated in ordinary life can help greatly to strengthen the true sense of self. The first of these is formed by taking care for the way in which one sees oneself. It is good to become accustomed to looking back over what one has achieved since memory first began until the present moment and to evaluate oneself on that basis. Such an evaluation is of course external. It does not include one's spiritual worth, which we would never be able to express adequately. The value of forming this habit of mind lies not in the evaluation of itself but in the inner strength produced by separating the hopes and fears of the heart from actual, outer events. Some people suffer from a continual sense of failure. My life has not been of much use, they feel, I could have made so much more of it. I have not made the most of myself and my opportunities. True humility and a wish to do everything that one does better in the future may prompt such an attitude. But it may well be that such a person has never accepted what he or she *has* actually achieved because their expectations were much higher than the reality which seems to them so meaningless. In order to form this habit of mind they will have to overcome the inclination to judge their lives against their hopes and ambitions. They may have to surrender some of the disappointment in doing so. Sometimes, there is a kind of inverse vanity in such despair about one's own existence, which will vanish with this habit of mind.

Other people, of more optimistic nature, are unable to distinguish clearly between what they have actually done and what they are intending to do. They speak so that the hearer can only imagine that they have begun great undertakings, until he discovers that the speakers were really talking of their plans. One of the temptations of living more and more vividly in ideas is that of becoming possessed by them, of handing them out to other people with an authority that is not justified either by what one has studied or carried out in practice. The safeguard against tendencies of this kind is the habit of recalling one's outer achievements correctly from time to time. There is no point in evaluating oneself spiritually by the measure of what has been outwardly achieved, of, for instance, taking a good salary as a sign of spiritual worth. But as an exercise, such a custom of mind has two great advantages. On the one hand it prevents tactlessness towards other people. From a spiritual point of view one may, for instance, understand much about the nature of certain illnesses. This is not a good reason for attempting to enlighten the minds of doctors and nurses, who have been looking after patients for years, unless, of course, an inquiry is made. On the other hand, it strengthens the inner awareness of the true self. The person who has practiced looking unemotionally at his outer existence becomes freer when he looks within himself to distinguish between his emotional personality and his true, lasting self.

Another habit of mind in daily life that fosters the strength of self needed for inner activity is conscientiousness in outer things. Sometimes people who become very interested in spiritual matters find conscientiousness in small things difficult. One of the reasons for this is that in the light of new ideals old standards can become meaningless. It is natural that a spiritually wakeful person cannot go on following customs simply because he was brought up to do so. He may have other interests than doing what his family wish of him. He may see through the absurdity of many government regulations. He may develop different moral feelings from those of the people in society around him. The quality of conscientiousness can help us through such problems. If such a person cultivates consideration of others, he will find it worthwhile to be punctual to appointments; if he takes as his ideal to cultivate an outer order that corresponds to his inner state, he will keep an account of his money, and keep order in his household. Then he will be conscientious in practical life in spite of the fact that he does not live by old, conventional standards. A conscientious person is much easier to live with, from the point of view of other people, than one who cannot be bothered about little things. He is a pleasanter person, from the point of view of the elemental beings, who occupy the things around us and are made angry by disorder. He is also a much stronger person in himself. He is not constantly confused by all the little things he has avoided, left undone or passed on to someone else. He leads a tidy life and can have a quieter mind, in which he can the more clearly experience the abiding self. An untidy outer existence is a hindrance to the inner life, while a tidy one gives it a calm background.

Those with an interest in the inner life are people who constantly try to bring the power of the spirit into their earthly existence. They realize that without it life is only half lived. Nevertheless, in our time great and active faith is required to continue patiently along this path. There is one fairly simple way of stimulating and encouraging this kind of faith. In a sense, all the three inner activities which have been described are doing this for us when we practice them. But it can be of value to describe in one thought, to which we can always return when we need it, how to revive our awareness of the spirit. We are accustomed to live our lives each in the setting and the circumstances provided by our personal destiny. Everyone has his place in the world, his relationships, his language and nationality. Many as are the muddles in such matters at the present time, some sort of framework of personal destiny belongs to everyone. Our feeling of personality depends very much on this setting. Some people are able to support the sense of themselves by what they have acquired in the course of life, by a house that they own, by a family gathered round them, by their profession or position in public affairs. Other people possess little or nothing to give them a sense of personal importance. Nevertheless, everything that personally belongs to us, that shapes our particular circumstances, is part of our experience of our personality. At the same time we are constantly being involved in limitations for this very reason. I cannot do that tomorrow, because I have promised to do something else, we are always saying. Right down to the people who cannot go away for a change of scene because they must not leave their garden or their cat, we are continually limited by our circumstances. Personality is a double-edged thing. While it gives us a satisfying sense of selfhood, it restricts us to a particular setting and a round of duties.

A further more serious limitation arises from personality. We are tied down by this force into ourselves and thereby cut off from the divine world. As much as we are aware of our personal interests, experiences and destiny, so we cut ourselves off from the universe of God. Our human task on earth requires us to be responsible for our personal destinies. It is of no value to try and escape from them. Yet inwardly, in thought, we can overcome the limitations of our personalities and this will strengthen our faith in the spirit. Today the attention of many people is constantly fettered to their personal concerns by anxieties. Difficult as it is to stop thinking of them for a while, they are in fact not made easier to bear by being too much in mind. Their solution is sometimes reached quickest when one is not thinking about them so much. It may be a good medicine even for anxieties to turn one's attention to thoughts which are not connected with personal concerns. Thoughts that are universally true, that are filled with moral goodness, bring the soul near to the divine world. They free the mind from the limitations of personality and make the human soul the companion of angels.

The most practical way to describe universal thoughts is to take mathematics as an example. In spite of all distinctions of race, dwelling place or profession, a triangle is the same for everyone. In the middle of a London street or an African jungle, the number three is the same. A square is a square from Arctic to Antarctic. Mathematical thoughts are not the only ones of universal validity. There are moral ideals of worldwide value. There are thoughts about the spiritual world that are true for people of every race. The problem arises at this point that we tend to experience such thoughts as vague generalizations. As such they are not much help to the inner life. When they are so carried in the mind as to become warm and living, concrete and exact, they bring the presence of the spirit very near. The parables in the Gospels enshrine many thoughts of this nature. Rightly understood, their meaning is true for all nations of people, over all parts of the earth. They are clothed in pictures so vivid and practical that they are not in the least vague. When faith in the working of the spirit and in one's own efforts at the inner life grows faint, then the mind should turn to a thought of universal truth and value. This brings the heart nearer to the world of the spirit and faith is revived and strengthened.

Concentration, contemplation, meditation and prayer are work for a lifetime. Yet they are not the kind of work of which one tires, for interest grows with experience. They are all directed to the main lifework of every one of us, becoming that which we are not yet. We have not become truly human, we are only on the way to fulfilling our existence. We know our aim, because Christ reveals in himself the ideal of man. In the light of this ideal, life is purposeful and filled with meaning. The duties of outer existence, the activities of the inner life, are the means that lead us towards our great end, becoming man in his true nature.

Part II

The Working of the Holy Spirit

The Holy Spirit in the Past and Today

We live in a time when the working of the Holy Spirit has changed and continues to change, and is coming through in a new form which we must strive to understand.

In the following chapters we shall try to explain why this study of *The Philosophy of Spiritual Activity* has the above title. We have to realize that the Holy Spirit has a history, for the divine world is not always in a 'constant state of being' but evolves. As a starting-point, let us try to consider the difference between the Father God and the Holy Spirit. Where should we think of looking to find the revelation of the Father God? In the universe in its created form, the earth under our feet, the world of nature, the stars above us, and in that part of us which is connected with these. Our physical bodies, our life-bodies, and, in a rather different way, what we could call the soul-body. Into this the Father God has 'sacrificed himself,' having 'fallen asleep' into creation, where he awaits resurrection or awakening. Thus it is a good thing to point out to young children the divine wisdom in the world of nature, in the construction of the body and the behaviour of animals, how we see a 'fatherly care' in their lives, the parental instinct being the greatest impulse in these. In all this we may see the working of the Father God. The Spirit God on the other hand is that part of the Cosmic spirit which has not been used up in creation, which is not present within creation. He is the unincarnated part of the Cosmic spirit.

If we use the term 'God' to indicate the whole Trinity, then God is in everything, but if we make the distinction between the parts of the Trinity it is as above. The sacrifice of the Father God has been made through and in the hierarchies, who are his hands and feet, ears and eyes — the members of his being.

There was a time when creation was still incomplete, and during this time a certain amount of inspiration could come from the Father God into human souls, the great example of this being the law of Moses. Rudolf Steiner called the giving of this law a 'geological inspiration,' for it came from the same forces that formed the rocks, from the 'sphere of form.' The law of Moses came, as it were, from underneath, as a part of the creative forces not used up in creation, and we can see a hint of this in the biblical wording, that the law was inscribed by the finger of God on tablets of stone.

But this kind of law gradually became impossible. The Greeks believed that the 'good' human being was the one who lived in accordance with the law of his nature: this 'law' also came from the sphere of the Father God. As this source dried up, inspiration had to come from above, from the sphere of the Holy Spirit. Before the coming of Christ, the Holy Spirit lived beyond the sphere of creation, so the question was how this influence was to reach human beings who were embedded in creation. Thus, the Egyptians believed that there was the Horus bird who brought inspiration from above. This can be seen in the statues of early Pharaohs, behind whose heads stands the bird, not easily visible from in front, whispering into their ears.

The equivalent in the Old Testament is the case of Elijah. If we read the story in the First and Second Books of Kings, it seems at first rather disjointed, but this was the way in which the writer of those days told something deeper than appears on the surface. Quite suddenly, we get the story of Naboth's vineyard, and of how Jezebel planned to get Naboth killed: after this had happened and Ahab had gained possession of the vineyard, he was sitting in it when Elijah suddenly came to him

and told him that he would die in the same place where
Naboth had died, and Ahab made the strange remark, 'Have
you found me O my enemy?' (1Kings 21:20).

The story is put in this form because Elijah and Naboth are,
in a sense, the same person, as Rudolf Steiner tells us, so that
the story of Naboth's vineyard is that of the death of the physical body of Elijah. It probably would have seemed wrong to
the writer of those days to give Naboth and Elijah the same
name, for while Naboth was the small-holder, Elijah was the
prophet, who would appear suddenly here or there, always
uttering the words which the Lord laid upon him. People saw
Elijah overshadowed with a great cloud of power, and would
not even be very clear what his physical appearance was like.
All the stories of Elijah are those of the spiritual experiences of
a man overshadowed by the Holy Spirit, who was so different
from Naboth, the owner of the vineyard, that no one realized
the identity between them except probably Jezebel, who was
deeply skilled in the mysteries of her own country.

It is hard at first to see why Ahab was so anxious to have this
particular vineyard, even though it did adjoin the royal property, so it looks as though we must regard it as a symbol for
something which Naboth had and which Ahab wanted very
badly. We hear that when Naboth refused to part with the
vineyard Ahab showed very great distress of mind. The way in
which Jezebel got rid of Naboth is also strange: she wrote to
the local notables asking them to invite him to a feast, which
they seem to have done gladly, and then arranged for two men
to bring false charges of blasphemy against him, so influencing
the people that they stoned him on the spot: thus she showed
great skill in working on people's emotions. Then, a little
while afterwards, Elijah appeared to Ahab in the vineyard and
told him, with the voice of the Lord, how he was to die.

At this time, Ahab was having the experience of Elijah after
his death, but Elijah had always been the unincarnated part of
Naboth, and therefore did not seem so different even though
Naboth's physical body was no longer there. Perhaps Jezebel

thought that by getting rid of Naboth's body she would also get rid of Elijah, but his story, in fact, goes on for a considerable while after this point.

After this, we come to a very interesting part of the story of Elijah, his last journey and reception into heaven. Elisha accompanies Elijah on this journey: they meet the 'sons of the prophets' and with these come to the River Jordan. Elijah parts the water with his mantle: he and Elisha cross over, but the 'sons of the prophets' remain behind and watch the subsequent events from across the water. Now Elijah asks Elisha what he would have as a parting gift, and Elisha asks that 'a double portion' of Elijah's spirit shall come upon him. But Elijah says: 'If you see me when I am taken, it shall be so, but if not, it shall not be so.' That is to say, it shall be given to him in proportion to his own spiritual stature. For if he were insufficiently developed, he would not be capable of receiving Elijah's spiritual power.

Then came the chariot and horses of fire, and carried Elijah up to heaven in a whirlwind: Elisha was able to see this, and Elijah's mantle fell down as he was carried away. When Elisha could see no more, he picked up the fallen mantle, and with this was able, in his turn, to part the waters of Jordan. And the sons of the prophets then accepted him as the successor of Elijah.

This was not really a physical experience at all, and an ordinary person, watching Elisha on his journey, would have seen nobody beside him. The water represents the etheric sphere, and the fire the spiritual world. Nor was it the physical body of Naboth which was received into heaven: this was already buried. But so strong was the etheric body of Naboth that this was still able to manifest itself for a considerable time until it had at last to be received into the spiritual world.

There was nothing in the human being of those days which could carry the Holy Spirit: the physical part had to be completely overshadowed by the mighty 'aura' of power. We need not consider that the Old Testament writer is concealing anything when he does not tell us that Naboth and Elijah were the same person, since Elijah was 'Naboth overshadowed by the Holy Spirit,' and therefore quite different.

If we go on to the New Testament, we find that the coming of Christ brings a great change in the relationship between human beings and the Holy Spirit. After the death and resurrection of Christ, the apostles and Mary are in the upper room, and the Holy Spirit descends on their heads in individualized tongues of fire, together with a sound as of a whirlwind. At this moment, the Holy Spirit descended from the spiritual world, making of the apostles the first community among whom he lived. This could only have happened because they were all together. For it is in the nature of earthly life that while such a great spiritual impulse can be received by individuals it cannot be kept except by a community. The apostles and Mary were 'twelve plus one,' as were King Arthur and his knights. Everyone can study and read at home, but we can better keep what we receive in a group. We may ask, in this connection, why most of Rudolf Steiner's work was done by means of lectures to small groups, not by books which could have reached much larger numbers with much less effort. This is because he had so many new things to say that he had to utter them to groups, for the readers of the books would read them in isolation, in their homes. By writing books he would have saved much travelling, but by lecturing to groups he was working according to the laws of spiritual life.

At no stage did the apostles imagine that they had received the Holy Spirit for themselves alone: they had to pass on the gift to everyone else. This realization was helped by the presence of Mary, who carried in herself something of the whole soul of humankind, the Mansoul of the medieval mystery-plays, and so represented the rest of humanity there. The apostles received the Holy Spirit in order that it should shine out from them.

But the relationship between the Holy Spirit and the apostles is different from what we find today. Nothing was done then without the guidance of the Holy Spirit, but this is manifested in strange ways, sometimes in dreams (as when St Paul was told to go to Greece), sometimes in a rather oracular form, through persons with 'gifts of prophecy,' who could give messages from the Holy Spirit which their companions could unerringly recognize as being genuine. Thus, though people had continual guidance, they received this through, but not out of, the human mind.

The exception was St Paul, who was 'born out of due time' and had a much more modern type of consciousness than his companions had. There was not generally present at that time the organ in the human being through which the Holy Spirit could work: he had come down, but still had to work as a 'companion,' from the outside and not from within.

The part which the Holy Spirit could directly use had not fully developed: the thinking capacity had not fully descended into human beings. This thinking capacity must not be confused with thought, which is merely the result of its activity. Until the tenth Christian century the thinking-capacity was still a cosmic capacity: only then did it became one fully in the power of human beings, and cease to be connected with the universe. When it did come down, there was something ready to receive it, the ego-consciousness brought by Christ, a spiritual capacity brought to us by him. But human beings were too weak properly to receive and use the gift, and 'devils' got hold of it first, producing materialistic thinking. Then, in 1879, the Archangel Michael began to unite himself with human thinking, to lift it so that it can be used by, and to make contact with, the Holy Spirit.

This lifting of human thinking is described in *The Philosophy of Spiritual Activity,* which is not really a 'philosophy' in the usual sense, but is really a description of the technique by which the consciousness can lift up the thinking-capacity so that this can be used by the Holy Spirit, which can thus directly enter human life. In the future, the Holy Spirit will not speak from outside, in dreams or in oracles, but when a true spiritual experience in one person meets a similar experience in another. Many people today still look for the Holy Spirit to provide a wisdom greater than we can produce for ourselves, but this was the old way. Nowadays we must not expect the Holy Spirit to do our work for us.

The new organ is that of thinking working in a new way, thinking in which a spiritual reality can live. But to produce this kind of thinking we have to do something about it for ourselves: we can no longer be just the 'carrier.' It is this process which *The Philosophy of Spiritual Activity* describes. This process is now possible for everyone, whereas in Old Testament days what happened to Elijah was only possible in a small number of people, for such an 'overshadowing' would have destroyed the bodies of most. But then, if you had the right constitution to be a prophet, you had to be a prophet, whether you wanted or not.

We have now to develop a kind of thinking which enables us to know what the Holy Spirit wishes of us, when we can obey, if we are willing to do so. We need not call it a 'very advanced' form of thinking, but it is a 'future' form, more perceptive and more imaginative, which occurs when we completely grasp the spiritual reality of something, not from material reasons. Thus we already know something about this kind of thinking, from our own experience.

Two Kinds of Thinking

We must now try to form a picture of this now kind of thinking before seeing how it comes about in *The Philosophy of
Spiritual Activity.* Let us take the facts we discussed in the last
chapter, and look at them from another point of view. We then
took the old kind of prophet in the person of Elijah, and the
working of the Holy Spirit as shown in the Acts of the
Apostles: let us now look at the process (not the form) of the
two cases, and the compare these with a passage from *Mysticism
and Modern Thought* by Rudolf Steiner.

We realized that a person who became a prophet in
earlier times had to live a completely double life. Thus,
when Elijah the prophet made his appearance, we find him,
as it were, 'coming from nowhere' and not being seen to go,
constantly surprising the people among whom he came.
Thus we see him recognized by Obadiah, who, however, did
not see him come or go. These people may have seen
Naboth, but did not recognize him as Elijah until he started
prophesying.

Elijah was not the only prophet of his time, but he was the
'unprofessional' one, who appeared on the scene because he
was inspired out of himself, whereas the majority of prophets
took it up 'as a career.' We may remember how Jezebel attacked
the prophets of Yahweh, when Obadiah saved a hundred of
them, whom he hid in a cave. These prophets lived, as it were,
in a 'college,' and it was the duty of this community of
prophets to keep open an organ of the soul through which
Yahweh could speak. But it did not follow that Yahweh would

speak through a member of the 'college,' and we see Naboth individually chosen.

People then knew of this kind of inspiration, and knew that every race had its proper god, but they did not expect to be more than recipients. The contest between Elijah and the prophets of Baal was a kind of 'international match': Baal was a true god, but belonged to another race. Alone, Elijah had to uphold Yahweh, whereas there were 450 prophets of Baal, and each side undertook to give a 'demonstration' of the power of its god. There is no doubt that Elijah believed that Baal was a real god (as we see from his taunting references to him), but Baal was not the right god for the Israelites. The people did not give Elijah any help or support, but awaited the outcome. They did not expect to choose for themselves, but expected something to be shown to them through the prophet.

Another story, showing how practically and directly the god worked through the prophet, occurs after Naboth's physical death. For a time, Elijah continued to have another 'life,' acting through his 'life-body,' an event which Jezebel had not reckoned with. The Lord sent Elijah to meet the messengers of the King of Syria, who were on their way to consult Baal at Akron, to ask them why they did not consult the God of Israel, and to say that the king would not rise from his bed but would die. The king then sent a captain and fifty soldiers to arrest Elijah: these, approaching him, were 'consumed by fire from heaven,' as were a second fifty. But the third captain to be sent begged Elijah to spare him and his men, and then Elijah came voluntarily with him to the king — but still told the king that he would die, and die he did.

Here we find Elijah 'sitting on a hill,' that is, a little above the world, for he then had no physical body (in spite of which the captains saw him). When the soldiers came too near, they came into the sphere of the life-forces, which affected them as though they had been struck by lightning. We are not told that Elijah attacked them, but they entered a sphere for which they were not prepared.

We may ask how people like Elijah got into such a state. He is like a man with a message to deliver: all his statements begin, 'Thus says the LORD,' and we may even ask whether he knew the content of the message until he came to speak it. This is rather the state of mind in which mediums work today. We could say that Elijah did not use his own human consciousness at all, but became an instrument, both in the use of his voice and even in the sphere of his will. We may remember how Moses had to veil his face after being near Yahweh. Thus, the personality of Elijah shrank to nothing when Yahweh over-shadowed him, and the message was that of Yahweh, to be delivered in the manner prescribed by Yahweh. When the Spirit of the Lord came on him he became nothing but an instrument, but people were then so well aware of this that the Spirit could have even external physical effects on others: it was then wholly external, with the same objective force as a thunderstorm, for example.

There are still people who would like to have the will of God act from outside as it did then. But what comes to them at such times may be no more than suppressed parts of their own selves speaking. For the Word of God no longer acts in this way.

In the Acts of the Apostles we see a great change, a good example being the story of Cornelius and Peter. Cornelius, a Roman soldier of Caesarea, 'a devout man,' saw a vision and heard a voice calling to him by name, as though to remind him of his individuality. Then the angel told him to send to Joppa for Peter, with full details of where to find him. Cornelius obeyed the quite practical instructions given to him, while the servants and soldiers seem to have accepted the situation as quite a normal one.

There is no more 'thus says the LORD,' but a kind of con-versation between two people side by side. At the same time, Peter had a complementary vision of the sheet lowered from heaven containing all manner of four-footed things, of which he was invited to eat. But he accepted this in so practical a manner that he could still raise his Jewish objections that he could not eat 'unclean things.' Then, when Cornelius' messengers arrived, he knew that his duty was to go and baptize the Gentile. We thus see the Holy Spirit still acting from outside, but reckoning with all the individual characteristics of the person addressed, and with their ordinary consciousness, like a companion.

Now, however, another change has happened, and we should be able to develop such a kind of thinking that something spiritual can happen in it. This is not 'logical thinking,' but a higher kind. In *Mysticism and Modern Thought* (p. 19), Rudolf Steiner tells us how the human soul can recognize itself from within by this kind of thinking.

> Thus self-perception implies self-awakening. In acquiring knowledge of things, we unite their being with our own. The message we receive from them becomes a part of our own self. The object that confronts me is no longed separated from me, once I have acquired knowledge of it. What I am able to gather from it becomes a part of my own being. If, now, I awaken my own self, if I become aware of the content of my own inner being, I also awaken to a higher plane of existence whatever I have made part of my own being from the world outside. The light that falls upon me at my awakening falls also upon whatever I have made my own from the things of the outside world. A light flashes within me and illumines me, and with me all that I have cognized of the world. Whatsoever I know would remain blind knowledge did not this light fall upon it. It would still be inadequate knowledge, though it encompassed the whole world, so long as it were not inwardly awakened to a higher mode of being. This awakening does not imply that the content of my knowledge is enriched by the addition of a new idea. Knowledge and cognition are raised to a higher level upon which all things are resplendent with a new light. So long as it is not raised to

this higher level, my knowledge remains, in a higher sense, valueless. The things of the world exist apart from myself: they have their being in themselves. What significance could there be in linking with their own independent being yet another (spiritual) being, which is merely a repetition of the things inside myself? If such a mere repetition were intended, it would indeed be senseless to enact it.

A mere repetition, however, can only be in question so long as I have not awakened, together with my own self, the spiritual content of things, and raised it to a higher level. When this occurs, I have not merely repeated within myself the being of things, but I have brought it to a new birth on a higher plane. With the awakening of my self, a spiritual rebirth of the things of the world is accomplished. What they then reveal was not previously inherent in them. A tree is there before me. I gather it into my consciousness. I cast my inner light upon what I have thus grasped. The tree becomes in me something more than it is outside. Whatever in it finds entrance through the gate of the senses is gathered into a spiritual content. A spiritual replica of the tree is within me, and I gather from it infinitely more concerning the tree than the tree outside can tell me. Then, for the first time, there shines forth from within me, towards the tree, what the tree really is. The tree is now no longer an isolated being in outer space. It becomes a member of the entire spiritual world that lives within me. It unites its content with other ideas that are within me. It becomes a member of the whole world of ideas that embraces the vegetable kingdom. It takes its place, further, in the graduated series of all things gifted with life.

The process of enlightenment described here begins with the sense of the spiritual reality within oneself and ends with the giving of spiritual reality to what is outside, so that a new kind of world can arise. Man can become a creative being. The Spirit of God works from within him.

The germ of life in this process is that of becoming spiritually aware of the spirit within ourselves. This is usually overlaid in us by another experience, that of our 'personality' or lower self, given to us through a form of experience which we can only have because we have a physical body. There is nothing wrong in this, only we experience it so strongly that the other is usually hidden. The experience of the self through the body can come through bodily exercise and sport, and this has become of the greatest importance in the West, which has its use in teaching us the sense of the bodily personality. We also sometimes see the 'sense of self' quite transformed when someone gets into their car, or owns property. Others have the experience in a more subtle way, such as when they have been present at some famous occasion, or become a patron of some society, or see their name on the front of a prospectus. This sense of earthly personality should not be despised, but we should *also* realize that we have the purely spiritual 'I' or ego within us, with which we can give spiritual reality to the world around us. This is described in the *The Philosophy of Spiritual Activity* as coming to us through the *activity of thinking* (*not* through 'thoughts' themselves): when we thus become conscious of the spirit within, we can bring to the outside world the spiritual reality which we have found within. The tree does not contain the 'idea,' but is only a 'copy of the idea,' and is waiting for something to come from us.

The kind of thinking which belongs to the earthly self gives *us* something, but the higher thinking can give something to the world outside. To think a living idea has an effect outside us and has a value for the universe. The other kind of thinking is necessary for us, for we could not live without it, but the higher kind is necessary for the world.

Let us try to form a picture of the difference between the two kinds of thinking: take, for example, a bird singing. We must disregard whether or not we like the singing, and approach it merely along the line of *how* we are going to think about it.

If we use the ordinary process of reasoning, we might ask; *why* does the bird sing? We may then produce all sorts of more or less reasonable answers, such as that the bird's song is a mating call, or that the bird is laying claim to certain territory.

To approach from the other direction, let us try to put aside all prejudices of our own personality, and form as clear and objective picture as possible of the bird singing. Then we should not ask *why* but *what* is the bird singing. We see the bird as an 'instrument for singing,' with singing as part of his nature and the singing of the various birds with some relationship between them. If we can see all the birds as a kind of choir, we can think of them as singing a song of the world's soul, expressed through them. Thus we may bring the living idea of the singing-bird to meet the bird. But we must remember that this same idea can also come down into the mere 'reasonable consciousness' and stand on a level with other opinions.

We can approach the idea of the being of the angels in the same way as that of the 'spiritual idea of the tree,' and thus form a bridge between faith and knowledge. With this form of knowledge we can pass from what is evident to the senses to what is not so evident, but is nevertheless real. We can observe angels, but in a different way from observing physical objects. If, for instance, we look back over the day at the 'accidents which just didn't happen,' we are entering the sphere of the activity of the angels. This is not so clear or manifest as the case of the tree or the bird. In these cases the living idea has to come from inside, and adds something to what we see with our eyes.

We can see this from another quotation from *Mysticism and Modern Thought* (pp. 22-25).

> Another example: I throw a stone in a horizontal direction. It describes a curve in the air and falls to earth. I see it in different places at successive moments of time.
>
> From this observation I learn that during its motion the stone is subject to various influences. If it were subject

only to my initial impulse, it would fly on for ever in a straight line without altering its velocity. But now the earth exerts an influence upon it. It attracts the stone towards itself. If, instead of throwing the stone, I had simply dropped it, it would have fallen vertically to earth and its velocity in falling would have continually increased. The mutual interaction of these two influences produces the phenomena I perceive.

Let us assume I could not separate in thought the two influences and by correctly combining them reconstruct, in thought, the phenomenon as I perceive it. In this case the matter would end with the ocular impression. It would be a mere gazing in mental blindness, a mere following of the successive positions occupied by the stone. But in actual fact the matter does not end there. The whole process is enacted twice over. Once, to begin with, outside — and there my eye sees it: then my spiritual activity causes the whole process to be repeated in a spiritual manner. The spiritual process, which my eye does not see, must be observed by my inner sense: it then becomes evident to the latter that I, by my own inner power, awaken the process for it to become spiritual.

We *do* use the higher kind of thinking, for example when we understand the working of gravity, but we are unaware of this and so do not realize that we could also use it for other purposes, for instance, to grasp something about the angels. We bring something from inside to meet something from outside — whether this be an object or an event — and combine them in the sphere of mental images. We all have the capacity now, but the question is whether we recognize it or not. Once we see the spiritual reality of ourselves from within, we have the possibility of seeing the spiritual reality outside ourselves.

There are two ways of experiencing the self within, either in moments of great crisis or by the use of the thinking capacity as described in *The Philosophy of Spiritual Activity*. In this,

Rudolf Steiner stresses the vital importance of realizing that there *is* a spiritual reality within us. In the days of Plato the ideas 'came down': now they should 'arise within us' and go out to meet the reality of the world. Thus we can resurrect the spirit which has 'died into' matter. This capacity for awakening the spiritual reality in ourselves has arisen since the beginning of the new Michael Age: it was not yet possible, for instance, in the age of Kant.

10

Thinking Free of the Brain

In the last chapter we tried to form a mental picture of the two kinds of thinking. Before beginning on the path which leads to this new kind of thinking, let us summarize the process. We can describe the change as one from 'it thinks in me' to 'I think.'

If we go back to the Greek philosophers, Plato and Socrates, we find that they did not have the experience 'I think,' but 'the world thinks and, if my mind is rightly directed, I shall receive these world-thoughts, so that they can live here on earth.' They sought to form an organ by which the world-thoughts could come to them on earth. So they did not have the same problem as we have of whether what they thought was true. To them, any healthy organ of thought would receive thoughts that were connected with reality, and therefore true.

We may remember that Socrates did not give lectures to his students: he held dialogues with them, often after dinner (a time which would be considered most unsuitable today). He started with the thinking which every one of them had, and showed him how to bring this nearer to the grasping of the world-thoughts. They did not have disputations or arguments. Instead, Socrates tried to develop their thinking into an organ which could receive the world-thoughts. Thinking was still a capacity for reception of inspiration.

But in the Middle Ages the conception 'I think' came in, and the characteristic of the training in medieval universities was 'disputations,' mental fencing-matches which may be compared with the physical contests of tournaments: the victors of the more important disputations, indeed, were honoured nearly as highly as were champions in the lists. These students used their thinking exactly as the knights used their weapons. There was now no suggestion that there were any world-thoughts which both disputants could share, but it was 'what I think' versus 'what you think.' Arguing always has something of this character. But now we are beginning to realize that argument does not bring us to the truth: it merely gives personal opinions. The medieval student felt that he had to defend his own thinking, which he expressed through his personality. So there was a kind of 'civil war of thought' in Europe, as was inevitable so long as this kind of thinking was used. For 'swords know no morals.'

Now it is our challenge to recognize once more that there really are world-thoughts, and that our thinking-capacity should be an instrument for allowing these to live in us in an individual way. The thoughts should live in us, but yet should be selfless. The thoughts of the Middle Ages were not selfless, but highly personal.

Something quite real happens in the human being when this change takes place from the thinking of the intellect to the thinking which is a vessel for the world-thoughts. What is to come about in future is something different from what happened in the past to Plato: now we should have selfhood without selfishness. When we attain this, we have altered something in ourselves, for the new thinking bears a different relation to the brain from the kind of thinking which we normally use for forming opinions.

We may now ask: what forces are we to use when we form this new kind of thinking? We use the same forces as children use for growing, the life-forces: only they do not use them for thinking. Normally, we think not *with* but *on* the brain. As the life-forces beat against the surface of the brain, like waves beating on the sea-shore, our thinking becomes conscious. For not all thinking need be conscious. Where the thought-forces meet the physical brain, consciousness arises.

We operate with *thoughts* in ordinary life, and do not often pay attention to the *thinking-capacity* which produces these. The kind of thought which developed in the Middle Ages has caused thought to become connected with the brain. What we have to do is to lift the life-forces away from the physical brain and use them in the sphere of the 'etheric head,' the sphere of life. We all do this in our more inspired moments, when we say that we 'have a brain-wave': we have then momentarily lifted our thinking away from the brain. When this happens, we surpass our limitations. For, when the life-forces can rise to the etheric head, they reach the sphere in which the world-thoughts are real.

The new kind of thinking should enable us to 'reach up and bring down brain-waves,' for it will no longer be 'deadened' by the brain. And *The Philosophy of Spiritual Activity* shows us the technique of this, so that our thinking can become 'morally inspired.' It will then become impossible for the thinker *not* to realize the moral implications of the decision being reached — whereas intellectual thinking need have no moral implications whatever. But spiritual realities are always connected with morality.

If, now, we look at the way in which *The Philosophy of Spiritual Activity* starts, we see that the path of experience described begins at a very definite point, with the capacity for asking questions, which is one of the most important capacities which we have at the present time. Rudolf Steiner has described how we have the sense of our own personality because our ancestors have developed this (especially in Western Europe), and how, as a result, we have lost our memory of earlier earth-lives, since we are so wholly taken up with our *present* personality. This sense of the personality has developed because of intense bodily experience. This emphasis on the importance of physical experience is reflected in many ways: in the interest in sport; the importance of having been present at an important occasion (with a body which can sit in a chair); the value attached to clothes (which only a body can wear), especially uniform. This sense of the personality had to be developed in the West, because it was the basis of the sense of the spiritual individuality. But it has been developed at the expense of interest in the world-thoughts, so unless something new comes in, the people of the West will be unable to take the next step. We must open ourselves to the world by asking questions. So this is a kind of historic moment, when we must open the new 'The Philosophy' with a question.

But we must ask the right question (for some questions are quite wrong and are mere caricatures). It should not be just a tiresome why-why-why? but should be an opening of ourselves, such that the answer will give us an extended view of the world, an enlarged experience. A really mature person will be less anxious to explain everything out of his own personality and will tend more to face the problems of life with questions, not ready-made answers. The nineteenth-century idea of a philosopher (as exemplified in Kant or Fichte) is a man who hands out the 'truths' which he has evolved out of his own thoughts. These were 'philosophies of statement': now we have to start not with a statement but with a question addressed to the human soul, on a line of inner development. It is one which anyone should be able to ask himself.

We see something of this foreshadowed in Eschenbach's version of the story of Parsifal and the Holy Grail. The whole crisis of this story is the question which Parsifal should have asked, but did not ask until much later. He had had no education in worldly things until an uncle took him in hand and taught him, amongst other things, that it was rude to ask questions. So he did not ask the meaning of his experiences in the Grail-castle until, long years after he had been cast out from it, he returned. The question which he should have asked the 'maimed king' was a very simple one — 'what is troubling you?' The whole story hangs on this simple question.

The opening words of *The Philosophy of Spiritual Activity* are: 'Is man in his thinking and activity a spiritually free being, or does he stand under the compulsion of an iron necessity purely conditioned by natural laws?' The wording of this question is the result of our modern scientific thinking, for it is only during the last few centuries that we have even had the concept of 'the iron necessity of natural law.' Socrates had no conception of such a thing. People had known that there were natural laws before the time of Galileo or Newton, but only after their time did it become a concept.

We must admit experiences of absolute necessity: thus, we feel hunger or the need for sleep, but do we experience anything else? Today, many people tend to regard *everything* as due to physical necessity as exemplified in the modern doctrine of 'hormones,' which are claimed to condition our thoughts, our mental state, our 'soul-life' and all. Such people say that if you don't believe them it is only because you 'don't know yourself.' There is no doubt at all that changes *can* be produced in us by hormones or other physical agencies, but are we to say, as a result, that there is nothing which is not so caused? This is a very vital question. If carried to its logical conclusion, the statement that there is indeed nothing that cannot be explained in this way would mean that no form of spiritual or religious life can have any real effect.

If we start from this question, it is clear that we must go on, not to an immediate answer, but to another question. At every point another vista opens up, inviting another question. *The Philoposophy of Spiritual Activity* is not a philosophy in the old sense, uttering authoritative statements: what is described is a technique for using our soul-forces. But at the time when it was written any serious book had to be written in a 'philosophical' style if it was to be noticed at all: hence the form adopted.

What we need is the capacity for asking questions and the use of our own common sense. And the asking of this opening question begins to open the way from 'I think' to 'it thinks in me,' because by it we open ourselves to receive the thoughts which can then live in us. Thoughts have created all the material world, but 'objects' have lost the living thought and have become mere 'monuments to thought.' But when we 'think them,' we can bring the living thoughts to meet the 'monument' and thus actually give back something to the world which was not in it before. If we think 'against the brain' in the old, argumentative way, it does not really matter what we think, but if we think the world-thoughts it really does matter what we think, for our thinking has an effect outside ourselves. We have thus to become responsible for our own thinking — and for its effect on the world outside.

What matters is not the *content* of the thought, but the thinking-capacity, the *way* we think. When we really 'think' for example a tree, we bring to meet the tree something more than was originally in it. And in order to do this, we must look at the tree with an attitude of question. Normally we tend just to look at a thing, recognize and 'label' it, and pass on, but if we can go beyond this, regarding its image in time as well as space, and ask ourselves what is its nature, we open ourselves to the possibility of receiving the real 'idea' of it. We must also suppress our own prejudices and personal reactions (such as whether we 'like it' or not), adopting a selfless attitude and letting it reveal itself to us. Then at last we may experience the 'idea' of the thing, which is quite different from our 'opinion of it.' But many people today hate the thought of any 'idea' which is not at the same time 'their opinion,' for then they feel 'unfree,' for such an idea would be connected with reality and they could not change it to suit themselves.

We can see very clearly the difference between the two kinds of thinking in the *Kon-Tiki* expedition. The builders of the raft had the 'idea' in real and living form, and took the greatest care to 'incarnate' it correctly, even to tying the knots with their own hands and insisting on using the correct kind of ropes, whereas their advisers put forward many plausible 'intellectual' reasons why everything should be done as 'they thought it should be done.' And had these 'reasons' been listened to the raft could not have survived the voyage. And when, at the end, the raft was lifted on to the deck of a ship, the thought which came to one of the party, that, whereas the raft had traveled 'with' the natural forces, the ship was 'in opposition to these,' expresses another living idea which was more than a mere personal opinion.

Freedom

We have spent some time contemplating the goal towards which we are going, in order to make it easier to find our way there. Now we must consider the mental processes required for covering the path to this goal, step by step. This will be in the nature of a quest and must be covered in sections, with limited aims to be attained one after another. The first of these aims is to be found in the middle of Chapter 3 of *The Philosophy of Spiritual Activity,* which gives the experience of the spiritual reality of the self and shows us the soul as a kind of casket, with a little treasure contained within it — the true self, which is not the same as the 'personality.'

We have already seen the great importance for people with the modern consciousness to be able to start from the capacity for asking questions, that is, for taking hold of our ego-force and offering it to be filled with spiritual knowledge. Thus, asking the right kind of question can be a holy act, the opening out of what has already developed within us.

Let us imagine ourselves as going on a journey of exploration, starting from the question with which the book opens: 'Is man in his thinking and activity a spiritually free being, or does he stand under the compulsion of an iron necessity purely conditioned by natural laws?' The first step consists of another question: is 'freedom' simply a matter of having the ability to choose between alternatives presented to us? No one who thinks really seriously about this can accept such a 'right of choice' as real 'freedom' — though this is just what most modern people do, as when they say, 'If I didn't have this or that obligation, I should be free!' For such a choice between alternatives, though superficially allowing some relaxation of the 'compulsion of iron necessity,' since it implies that we are not compelled by obligations to act in one specified way, would still depend on, and be limited by, the range of external alternatives presented to us.

Take as an example that we have a certain sum of money to spend, and go into a shop. We can 'choose' what we shall buy — within the limits of the larger or smaller stock available there. We thus have 'freedom' to choose between a set of possible actions already decided by the existing circumstances, but we depend in the last resort on something outside ourselves. But this is just what very many present-day people believe that freedom is, and they assume this in their ordinary activities of life.

Thus, we have to take our next step towards 'freedom,' as something more than a mere 'opportunity to choose between alternative circumstances,' much as we may enjoy the power to do this. Freedom has to be created: the mere fact that we have, for instance, to go to work at a certain time and place need not rob us of freedom, though it must be accepted that there are many situations in life in which freedom is not possible.

The steps followed up in Chapter 1 of *The Philosophy of Spiritual Activity* do not purport to be a history of philosophy: they merely present a series of experiences by different philosophers, which are of value, not for their own sake (for all are shown to be true only up to a certain point) but as illustrating steps which have to be faced and overcome if we are to progress beyond them. Thus, Rudolf Steiner starts with David Friedrich Strauss, who 'attempts to develop a new faith out of the results of recent scientific research' and who says, 'The alleged freedom of indifferent choice has been recognized as an empty illusion by every philosophy worthy of the name.' Steiner continues with Herbert Spencer, who states that, 'Everyone is at liberty to desire or not to desire: which is the real proposition involved in the dogma of free will, is negated

— by the analysis of consciousness.' According to this point of view, there is always, so we are told, a perfectly definite reason why, out of several possible actions, we shall carry out just one and no other. We shall, in fact, follow our disposition and shall therefore make one particular choice, not really being 'free to choose' at all.

But something has been overlooked here. If everything we did really was predetermined in this way, we should never make use of our conscious thinking, as opposed to our instinctive impulses. For we can, if we wish, deliberately go against what we should like to do: we can, if we try, do something to 'change our disposition.' There is something else in us, beyond what Strauss and Spencer can see.

Next, Rudolf Steiner quotes Spinoza, who had progressed a step further than Spencer. Spinoza says, 'Thus I call that thing "free" which exists and acts from out of the mere necessity of its nature, and I call that "under compulsion" which is constrained as to its being and action by something else, in a precise and fixed way.' For Spinoza, therefore, freedom consists 'not in free decision but in free necessity.' God, for example, is free because he 'exists only through the necessity of his own nature.' An excellent modern example of this point of view is Woodrow Wilson's definition of freedom: 'a ship running freely before the wind' or 'a piston moving freely in a machine,' with the admission that if the ship tried to run against the wind it would become 'unfree.'

Spinoza gives as an example the case of a stone thrown through the air and then following a path 'defined by the thrust of an external cause.' 'What is true here for the stone,' says he, 'is true also for every other particular thing, however complicated and many-sided it may be, namely that everything is necessarily determined by external causes to exist and act in a fixed and definite manner.' The onlooker, he points out, knows that the stone owes its motion to the fact of its having been thrown, but he imagines that, if the stone 'during its motion thinks' it could assume that it was choosing to move in its predetermined course. According to Spinoza, then, human beings think that they are free because they do what they want to do, but they do not realize the compelling force of their own wants. He then quotes the example of a baby crying for food, that of a small boy fighting, the utterances of a drunken man. But, in all these examples, the urge undoubtedly is due to natural causes, arising out of the necessities of our nature, and therefore, admittedly, none of them is a free action. But Spinoza has overlooked the fact that human beings are not only conscious of their actions but may also become conscious of the causes of their actions. He has put into the same category the motives for all human activities, whether it be a baby crying for food or a soldier who sacrifices himself to save his comrade on the battlefield.

Instinctive impulses undoubtedly do happen in us, and these, insofar as they remain merely instinctive, depend on 'iron necessity.' But we also perform conscious activities, being aware of the motives guiding us, and in these we can be free. Spinoza has put everything into the unconscious sphere. Indeed, a larger proportion of our actions than we usually think can be placed into this sphere, not only what arises out of our organic needs but also everything which we do without thought, everything which we do because we were 'brought up that way' or because it has 'become a habit.' An identical action may be performed by two people out of entirely different backgrounds: one may offer his seat in a bus because instinctive politeness has been 'built into him,' while in another it is a conscious act prompted by the particular circumstances. All of us have a part of our character formed already, in which we do behave like instinctive beings, and thus not 'freely.' We must thus make the important distinction, which Spinoza failed to see, between motives which are instinctive and those of which we are conscious.

Now Rudolf Steiner goes on to Eduard von Hartmann, who says that it is easy to believe that we have a part of our nature which is free, but that we shall see all our actions as the result of a meeting between the necessity from outside (circumstances or 'destiny') and that from inside (our character). He says that when, for example, it is our 'destiny' to enter a shop with money to spend it is our 'cast of character' which decides which of several possible things we shall buy. Thus Hartmann says that, even when our motives are conscious and when we think that we are making free decisions, we always, in fact, act in accordance with our character.

But, to be thus, we should have to be beings of fixed character, never changing unless external circumstances altered us. In fact, Hartmann has given an excellent description of the 'human personality,' while ignoring the fact that there is a part of us beyond this. The part which Hartmann describes is actually a very large part of us, because it includes what we have received from upbringing, inheritance, and even karma. But this part of us can never be free: it is the part in which 'results work.' If one could get a reliable horoscope cast, showing all the influences acting at the time of birth, and if the whole of life then ran in accordance with this forecast, one should not be pleased but should ask what had gone wrong. For what we shall subsequently achieve out of ourselves, in freedom, cannot be written into the horoscope. Hartmann, however, describes just that part of us which can be written into the horoscope — but nothing more. He could see no solution to his own riddle, and his final conclusion was that all wise men should agree to mass-suicide, so as to bring the human race to an end.

But how do we escape from this? Even though we must admit that a very large part of what we do is motivated by our character, in its widest sense, as we can see by taking a trip abroad and observing how much we depend on national characteristics, we must realize that this is not all. There are 'two people' in us, the 'personality' (which Hartmann has described), and another part which is outside this and which can *change our character.*

Now Rudolf Steiner asks whether there is not a difference between a conscious motive and an unconscious instinct, and how we are to know whence our motives come. This leads us to the realization that we have to think of the human being who can act out of conscious knowledge. Hartmann has separated the human being who thinks from the human being who acts. Hartmann the 'thinker' looks at Hartmann the doer (referred to as 'the human being'), and says that this other human being is acting from necessity. So long as he says that 'the human being' does this or that, he is making his thinking self into an onlooker, quite unconnected with the actor. Had he said: '*I* am acting as a result of my character,' he might have realized how he was dividing himself into two parts. In order to follow his line of thought, however, he refers throughout to 'you' or to 'the human being,' and never asks himself: 'But who is it who is thinking like this?' The two parts into which the human being has been divided never meet, and the human being who 'acts because he knows' is ignored. Such thinkers do not expect to act out of the same kind of thinking as they have used in order to observe the 'actor.' But we have to realize that we can act out of the same forces as we use for this activity of observation, and that then we should no longer be acting out of mere necessity. When we begin to use this power of thinking we can produce motives which are not already 'built into us.' We then stand at the beginning of the development which leads to freedom.

We find very many present-day scientists thus describing the human being by the use of forces when they subsequently deny that the human being possesses. Thus they describe him as a machine, but in order to do so they use forces of thought such as no machine ever had — and the same applies when they describe him in animal terms. This is a basic error underlying all materialistic world-conceptions: these bring forward a train of thought, but then deny the validity (in other human beings) of the very process which has been used to establish theory. Thus, if we observe the thinking human being, we see in him those very forces which Hartmann denies in others when he ignores the 'man who acts because he knows.'

Having seen this, we may go on to ask: with what forces do we bring about the motives for our decisions? And how are we to distinguish between those which we consciously bring about and those which we do not? The whole point is not whether we are able actually to carry out the decision, but out of what forces the decision could ever arise. This leads to the experience of thinking as the force by which conscious motives are brought about in us.

From this we can get an idea of what human freedom means. The personality, much as we value it, much as we do and must use it, is not free, for it is the result of all that has happened in the past. But it is not in this that our spiritual reality lies, and it can be changed by our efforts. It is the power of thinking which opens the way to spiritual reality in ourselves, and the motives produced by this thinking are the ones leading to freedom. Many people value their feelings more highly than their thoughts, but actually all real feelings (apart from instinctive ones) have their origin in thoughts, especially the nobler feelings. 'The heart and the mood of the soul do not create the motives. They presuppose these and let them enter. The way to the heart is through the head.'

Love is no exception — if by love we mean something more than the mere expression of sexual instincts. One cannot really love another person in whom one has not seen, in thought, something beautiful. The first step is in thought. It is not that love makes us blind to the other's faults, but that it opens our eyes to what is beautiful and worthy of respect in the loved one, but which was not seen before or by others. One can feel 'sympathy' instinctively, or parental affection, but not higher love which contains spiritual reality.

We must be clear that it is the forces we use which matter, not the actual action. Thus, the attempt to *become tidy* is of spiritual value, but once this has been done and the habit of tidiness becomes instinctive it has become a part of us, no more than a picture of our past. There is then no spiritual value in mechanical tidiness *as such,* but there is spiritual value in the 'creation of order.' So, when the achievement is complete, we should not be content just to rest on the ground we have won, but, while taking care to retain this, we should turn our efforts to achieving something new.

12

Observing Thinking

We have now come to the point where we have to decide that we can only advance further by investigating our own thinking. We saw that, in any action, the important part is the motive, the process by which the action was arrived at, and that we have to distinguish between those motives of which we are conscious and those of which we are not. But now, in following up the *The Philosophy of Spiritual Activity,* we appear to deviate from the straight course, for Chapter 4, though it does lead us further into the nature of thinking, does not at first sight appear to do so.

First, however, we should consider what we really mean by 'thinking' in this connection, for we are accustomed to use this word for several different things. We use the word so loosely that very often it does not mean real thinking at all. We must, for a start, distinguish between the activity of thinking and the thoughts which are the result, the end-product, of this activity, for what is important is how we come to the thoughts. The activity of thinking is a highly spiritual process, on a level far above that of many of the thoughts which are produced by it. The level of the capacity, however, is not lowered by what we do with it, though our thoughts are by no means always worthy of the process by which we think them — and more so than ever in modern times. For in old times the cosmic thinking which came down into human beings was under the protection of Michael, until, in about the tenth Christian century, the thinking 'came down into human beings,' who became able to use it for whatever purpose they wanted, however trivial or materialistic. But what we usually notice most, if not entirely, is merely the thoughts, the result of the process of thinking.

Another thing which we have to notice is that much modern 'thinking' consists of no more than the combination of existing thoughts, arranging these logically, putting them in connection with one another, and thus drawing conclusions from them. But this is not thinking in the sense here meant by Rudolf Steiner. Logic is only the force of natural law an earth working in thought, the form which the conditions of earthly life require. But the kind of thinking described in *The Philosophy of Spiritual Activity* has to do, not with arranging thoughts, but with producing them. When we consider the thinking-capacity, we must realize that the thought, in the final form in which we can pass it on to others, is only an end-product. At a stage before this, we can put the thought into words for ourselves, but not yet for others. Still earlier comes the stage where we have formed a mental picture, for which we have not yet found words. And, still earlier than this, we 'think,' even before the thought incarnates sufficiently to enable us to form a picture.

Many people are not aware of their thinking until they get to the pictorial stage, or even to that of words. The thinking before the picture form is really 'outside time,' but this and one or more of the later stages may seem almost simultaneous. The 'thinking before the picture' stage may even seem like a kind of blank. It is the real self which carries out this activity, of which we are not aware until it enters consciousness. If we can stop the 'talkative,' worrying kind of thinking, with which we so often turn a subject over and over in our minds, we may give the real thinking-capacity a chance — as we see when the solution of some problem comes to us after a period of calm reflection, even after a time spent actively on something else. Thinking, then, is a spiritual activity carried out by ourselves, which in its last stages becomes words — but these are only like the apples produced after the year's work on the part of the tree. But 'putting apples together in a bowl' is not real thinking.

We find that Chapter 4 of *The Philosophy of Spiritual Activity* starts from 'my experience of the world around me.' As human beings, we are never satisfied, never completed, by the world around us: we are always asking for more and find ourselves asking questions about the world with a kind of mental hunger for what the word has not given us. Only when we are asleep are we satisfied with the world around us, for all we need is given to us then. When we are awake, we cannot be thus satisfied, though the animals and plants are able to live entirely out of the world around. Nature does not provide us with all we require, either in the material or the psychological sense: it provides us with things which we can see and hear and touch, but it does not offer us the explanation, the ideas behind the things. After death, however, we shall understand everything we perceive, by the very act of perceiving it, while we shall not perceive what we do not understand: thus, those without spiritual thoughts will then feel themselves in a blank, even though the whole cosmos is around them. But this is a kind of perception entirely different from what our senses give us on earth.

Here we see the world: we are aware that we have a connection with it, we see in ourselves counterparts of what is happening in nature, and yet we feel ourselves separated from it. 'The something more which we seek in things, ever and above what is immediately given to us in them, splits our being into two parts. We become conscious of our opposition to the world.' But the separation is brought about by us, not by nature. It is brought about by our consciousness, for we find that we have to add our thoughts to the world outside, and these thoughts come to us from inside, not from outside ourselves. We are constantly separating ourselves from the world and then joining the two parts together again by means of our thoughts, and thus we become conscious of ourselves.

This duality has been an insoluble problem to philosophers for centuries, whether they speak of 'spirit and matter,' 'subject and object,' 'thinking and appearance' or any other pair of terms. Some called themselves dualists, paying attention only to the separation between the 'I' and the 'world,' and having to admit, after long efforts, that they could not bridge the gap between the two. On the other hand, the monists, paying attention only to the unity, tried to bridge the gap in several ways. The (philosophical) materialists said that the only 'reality' was matter, and that all 'spiritual activity' comes about as a result of material processes — as we see in the hormone theory of behaviour. This school would make thinking entirely dependent on material processes in the brain, and thus conditioned by such considerations as what we ate for lunch.

On the other hand, the (philosophical) spiritualists, or idealists, claimed that spirit is the only reality and that matter is only an 'appearance.' In its extreme form, this school would declare that an empty room would simply cease to exist until someone came into it who could perceive it. This is the basis of Christian Science.

A third school of monists assumes a kind of reconciliation, declaring: I see the world and have my mental pictures of it, but I cannot be sure that what I see has a reality behind it. This, however, does not answer the question, but merely pushes it a stage further back. However, it does lead us on to the next step. This standpoint admits that there may be a real world behind what I perceive, perhaps quite different from this. But I have to work with what I can perceive, and so must remain within the boundary-wall imposed by my own consciousness, while 'reality,' lying beyond the wall, remains incomprehensible to me. This is the standpoint of Kant, and of the Catholic Church, which says, however, that certain rays of truth (revelation) can reach us from beyond the wall, but that human thinking could never have attained to the content of these revelations unless these were given to us by God. It is as though we were walking in a walled park, unaware of the country outside, which may be quite different from what we perceive inside the wall.

We get over this difficulty by the experience described in
Chapter 5, for here we discover a source of reality in ourselves,
by which we can then judge the reality of the world. We have
now returned to the straight path, and ask what part our thinking plays in the activity which we perceive in the world. If, say,
we watch the motion of a billiard-ball, which moves until it
strikes another, both then moving in new directions, we may
watch, as mere unthinking observers, seeing the successive
positions of the balls. Then we have no inkling of what will
happen after the impact, and if we looked away just before this
point we should be entirely unable to say what was going to
happen. As soon as we wish to forecast what will happen, or to
see a connection between the successive events, we must
engage in thinking and bring our judgment to bear on what we
perceive. The event is taking place without our being involved,
and will take place in the same way whether we observe or
reflect on it, or not, but now 'I try to add to the occurrence
which takes place without my assistance a second process
which takes place in the conceptual sphere. This latter process
is dependent on me.' The connection is not supplied by the
outer world, but by ourselves, even though the process may be
so rapid that we believe it to be inherent in the objects and
processes perceived. It is thinking which supplies the connection between percepts and processes which are really, so far as
our 'unthinking perception' is concerned, separate and unconnected. We may even 'combine phenomena in advance' in
thought, and then imagine for a while that we are perceiving,
next, what we expected to perceive, until clearer observation
shows that we are wrong.

When we turn our perception to our 'inner landscape,' we
really have the same relationship with this. Even here, we still
have to provide thoughts in order to be able to see the connec-
tions. We can look on what is occurring inside as at a landscape: our feelings and our will-impulses come to meet us as
objects of observation, but our thinking is found to be different. It is possible to observe, say, one's feeling of anger against

someone in the same way as one observes the object of the anger: the feelings are 'inner objects,' but nevertheless objects. We feel more strongly and more personally about these inner objects, but we have the same relationship with them in the consciousness. Actually, we look both inwards and outwards at once, without realizing this, but, as regards the self which is observing, we are really in the same relationship, whether or not we judge the object more subjectively.

But with our thinking (not our thoughts) it is different. The thoughts are objects, as the result of thinking, but the thinking, which we do ourselves and in which our whole self is involved, cannot be observed at the time, but only afterwards, just because the whole self is involved *in* the thinking. Then, by observing 'ourselves engaged in thinking,' in retrospect, we can at last see a reality present in the self. We are now no longer within the walls of the park: we can look out through the gate and observe the reality of the self in activity — for this, at last, is something 'real.'

People may object that there is no difference between this and what happens when observing the feelings or the will. The self certainly is in these, but in our feelings the self is in a 'state of dream.' We observe ourselves as feeling, but do not observe our selves as active in the production of this feeling, and the same applies to the will, in which the self is in a 'state of sleep.' But we can look back on the self as a thinking being, not merely on the thoughts produced but on the self producing the thoughts. This is not a normal activity: 'we must be quite clear that, in observing thinking, we are applying to it a method which is our normal attitude in the study of all other contents of the world, but which in the ordinary course of that study is not usually applied to thinking itself.'

This was something which the earlier philosophers could not do. The reason why it escapes us is that usually we do not look behind the later stages in the process of thinking, the words or the picture, to the stage where we may observe the self thinking. In this activity, which goes on before the picture is formed, the self is active. It may be hard to see this; we know, however, that such an activity has happened, and if we hold to this it may quite suddenly come to us. But when we do reach this point we have access to the reality of the world, and have overcome the difficulty which the philosophers could not solve — partly because an evolution of consciousness has taken place since 1879 which makes us able to attain to what they could not.

It we succeed in observing 'ourselves thinking,' we shall discover, not the 'personality' which is all we observe if we look at 'ourselves active in the feeling and the will,' but the real self. From this point we can advance further. We shall have acquired a new relationship with the self: we shall be aware of the process which we have hitherto used without being aware of it. After this, the spiritual world can become real to us.

13

Active Thinking

One of the experiences which many people have nowadays is the feeling that they ought to be living on what is provided for them (which includes not only the financial aspect, but also the gifts of their own minds), yet they find that they cannot do this. Thus, they would like to see without the effort of looking, to hear without the effort of listening. They think that a place should be provided for them in the world, and that they should be able, amongst other things, 'just to think,' without the need to do anything for themselves in the matter. We find that many people are coming to a point where they are no longer using their eyes and ears properly. Young people, especially, are tending in large numbers to lose all hold over their own soul-forces. We can see how few, today, have retained any real sense of logic, any real healthy appreciation of the laws of the earthly world.

We have, in fact, reached a point at which a whole new stage in the evolution of human faculties needs to come about, but this time, unlike what has happened in the past, it will not happen unless we do something about it for ourselves. Unless we make an effort, we are in danger of losing our ability really to use our eyes in the outer world. In this connection, we may note how ever more natural, ever more elaborate presentations are offered to us, for instance, by the cinema, in which the sense-impressions come to meet us, so that little effort is required for watching them: one need hardly look at all. But, in real life, the more we look, the more we see. We have to 'use our eyes' in order to get the benefit of what is around us, and it may be truthfully said that we probably see far less than people did fifty years ago.

Nowadays, our faculties will no longer just 'function in us,' and if we want to keep them we must use them. If we 'put our mind' into our looking, and concentrate, we shall see quickly and correctly. The question now is, how to use our minds not only to develop but even to keep our faculties. In this connection, we may note how colour-blindness and tone-deafness are on the increase today.

The same thing is happening with the faculties of the human mind, and it is generally accepted that people do not think as well, now, as they used to do. Nor does modern education teach children to think: they are simply stuffed with other people's ready-made thoughts until their heads are addled, with no time or opportunity to think about these for themselves. Generally, the kind of thinking with which we have to deal in modern life is in a form which somebody else has worked over, handed to us as a finished product, to be accepted without further thought on our part. But now we have to consider how to make a further step for ourselves.

In life, we are usually dealing with the products of the mind, and seldom concern ourselves with how the mind works. But, until we do acquaint ourselves with the working of the mind, we are not well-equipped for producing anything new with it. The point, then, from which we have to advance is the realization that, if we can 'get behind our thoughts' to the activity of thinking, we find what at first sight seems like a blank but in which we can find the self active in the production of the thoughts. But this is not what we usually refer to as the 'self,' which is merely the 'character,' a collection of personal qualities. If we try to judge these qualities of ours, this 'character,' we shall find it very hard to form a fair judgment, but there is one place where we can find a really true picture of the self — and this is in the activity of thinking.

We must make ourselves aware of the different relationship in which we stand in respect of our thinking and of all our other soul-activities. We can only observe the forces of the will or of the feeling, but we can actually observe ourselves (in retrospect) active in the thinking. Sometimes, too, we can feel the force of somebody else's will bearing on us — whether we resist this or submit to it. But we cannot tell how this force is produced. We have no conscious experience of will until it has become a force with which we have to reckon. The relation of the self to the will is thus that we experience a will-force, which we can handle and (to some extent) control, but that we have no experience of its origin.

In the case of feeling, we do not feel a 'force' like this. Feelings are more fluid than will: we can get held of them more clearly and we have some power of choosing between them. We can act on the will by means of the feelings, but not directly by means of the thoughts, unless some element of feeling comes between. But when we come to consider how feelings are produced in us, a good approach is to consider how hard it is to change a feeling 'to order,' or to rid ourselves of it. When we succeed in doing this, the feeling 'leaves us': it has departed out of us. Feelings enter us and go out again. And examples may be quoted to suggest that the feelings expelled from one person may actually pass into someone else, as when the quietening of one patient in a mental hospital ward may be the signal for a similar outbreak in another patient, or several such outbursts, perhaps, following one another in succession. The forces of feeling 'flow into us,' we have some degree of control over them: we can expel them, but we cannot say, as in the case of thoughts, that we see ourselves producing them. If we are very angry, we may feel that 'anger is shaking us,' as though it were an external force. And we may note the truth contained in the old phrases, 'fear came upon me,' 'anger took hold of him,' and so forth. The answer to the problem posed by the expulsion of feelings from ourselves is that we should not expel them: our souls should be places where unsuitable feelings are transformed, not from which they are expelled, perhaps to work harm elsewhere.

In the saying, 'I will not entertain such a thought,' we have a combination of feeling and thought. We have a dislike of the bad thought: if we had been able to see as far as the birth of the thought, the thinking-activity, we should be in a better position to do something about it, but by the time the thoughts have reached the stage of words our relation to them has changed. They are now 'objects,' just as is the feeling about them. But we *have* produced the thoughts in a way quite different from what we can say of the feelings and of the will. If we look at our inner landscape, we shall find will-forces coming from we know not where, feelings coming and going, and thinking which we can see that we produce for ourselves.

The important point is to keep clear our picture of the stages by which a thought is born. 'The first observation which we make about thinking is that it is the unobserved element in our ordinary spiritual life.' There is something in this 'blank before the picture' akin to the 'chaos' before the beginning of creation, as told in Genesis, with the self active in this 'creative chaos.' 'The reason why we do not notice the thinking which goes on in ordinary life is that it is caused by our own activity. Whatever I do not myself produce appears in the field of my consciousness as an object: I contrast it with myself as something whose existence is independent of me. It comes to meet me. I must accept it as the presupposition of my thinking. As long as I think about the object, I am absorbed in it, my attention is turned to it. To be thus absorbed in the object is just to contemplate it by thinking. I attend, not to my activity, but to its object. In other words, while I am thinking, I pay no heed to my thinking, which is of my own making, but only to the object of my thinking, which is not of my making. There are two things incompatible with each other: productive activity and the contemplation of it. The thinking must be there first, if we are to observe it.

We may ask whether it is possible to miss out any of the stages in the normal process of producing a thought. It is. For in the production of much modern, abstract thought, the 'mental picture' stage is omitted. And we may remember that Rudolf Steiner has told us that the English-speaking peoples have the special task of developing the consciousness soul, which is particularly concerned with the formation of mental pictures. We can often test the reality behind someone else's thought by trying to form a mental picture of its content, and very often we shall find ourselves quite unable to form one.

There is a particular danger connected with this, for while what we perceive in the world (the 'percept') and the 'concept' which comes to meet it from within, should, if properly observed and formed, be free from error, the sphere of our mental-pictures does contain the liability to error. Thus, it is important that our mental pictures should be connected with reality, for if they are not they can lead us into any folly and unreal abstraction of our own building. If we realize this, and seek to connect other people's thoughts, as well as our own, with reality, we shall be better able to resist propaganda. We may ask why the Germans, many of them highly intellectual people, accepted Nazi propaganda and 'slogans' so easily: this was because they had neglected their capacity for thinking for themselves.

One of the greatest errors of the present day is to work entirely in the sphere of our own mental pictures, and to treat these as the only reality. For then we become entirely divorced from reality. An excellent example of this is what actually happened to a doctor in charge of a hospital on the west coast of Scotland, to whom patients from the islands, sometimes in urgent need of operations, came from time to time by steamers which arrived as tide and weather and other circumstances dictated. Such operations were, of course, performed as soon as the patient arrived, irrespective of what else was on hand. Then came the National Health Service, when a directive arrived from Whitehall that, henceforth, operations were only to be performed between 9 am and 1 pm on Mondays to Thursdays. A protest from the doctor that neither the steamers nor the patients could be expected to fit themselves into this arbitrary arrangement of the doctrinaire 'planners' was met by the statement that 'statistics had showed' that the necessary quota of operations could be performed within the hours proposed, and that the directive must be adhered to!

The 'personality' will not give us a point of true reality from which to start our further investigation, but the true self, as observed (in retrospect) in the activity of thinking, is such a point of reality, from which we can go on to consider the reality of our percepts. In the stage of thinking before the mental picture, we find an activity in which the self is occupied. This part of our being is at present like a seed, and if we would find it we must 'dig for it,' but it has to open out to become a vessel for the truth of the world to enter. Then it will be raised to the level of Inspiration, and can be used by the Holy Spirit. And, once we have get hold of the self, we can begin really to use the thinking capacity.

14

Mental Pictures

We have something in the foreground of our consciousness which we have got to get behind: this is the life of mental pictures. If we can see how these come about, we shall see how we can get outside the world which we make for ourselves, which is personal to ourselves. The German word for a mental picture is *Vorstellung. Stellen* is to stand or place something, so that a literal translation of *vorstellen* would be 'to place something before [something else].' Thus a *Vorstellung* is what one places in front of oneself. In the same way, a *Wahrnehmung* is what we perceive, a 'percept,' while a *Begriff* is the concept inside us, which comes to meet the percept and, where these meet, gives rise to the mental picture, the thought.

Normally we tend to work entirely in the sphere of our own mental pictures, which fill our consciousness in ordinary life. They are part of our subjective life: we need them in life and use them, but they take up too much of our mental space. We have mental pictures not only of things in the world outside, but also of the things of our own inner world, such as our own feelings. If, for instance, someone mentions a thing which we dislike, we get a mental picture of the dislike at the same time as that of the thing: perhaps the mental picture of the feeling precedes or even takes the place of that of the thing. Memory works in mental pictures of this kind, but it would be wrong to say that all mental pictures are of the nature of memory. But the mental pictures which we carry with us are our own little inner world, containing what we have experienced both inside and outside. They are private to every one of us, yet they are constantly before us. We live in them and do not share them with others, and therefore we all have a tendency to egotism. We may even get our percepts wrong, because we confuse what we actually see with what we think we ought to see, to fit our already-existing mental pictures. We see others through our mental pictures, and every one of us works with his own little inner world, inside and extending around ourselves.

If a more experienced person meets a less experienced one, and speaks of something which the other has never experienced, it is often very difficult to share the mental picture with him. Sometimes this can be done by finding a point in common from which a start can be made — but this must be a point within the mental-picture-world of the other. In such a case one must 'get outside one's own skin' and get inside the world of the other's mental pictures — as is most evident in teaching. If we try the experiment of trying to enter the world of someone else's mental pictures, we begin to realize how personal our own are. But we can, nevertheless, change our mental pictures: indeed, we must keep doing so. We may, for instance, meet very old people who have a very rich store of mental pictures but who have not changed them for a very long time: such 'fixed mental pictures' tend to become ever stronger until they become more real, to the person, than the actual reality of the world. Such people then become gradually more and more out of touch with reality, and live in a world of their own, perhaps in a past age, decades ago.

We can see how these mental pictures work. The point which is usually overlooked in connection with this world of mental pictures is not that they are our own, subjective world, but that we have made them ourselves. We can only have a healthy relationship with them if we realize this, and that we can, and should, change them. Our consciousness is limited. We cannot have the whole of the big world in our own little world, but we can have some of it, and if we want to have more we are able to 'stretch the container' to hold more: it is not like a cupboard which, when full, will held no more. What makes us feel that we are too overcrowded with thoughts is that we do not become masters of our mental pictures: we let ourselves be chased about by them. But if we become master we can afford to extend the boundaries of the consciousness.

We always want to make our inner world fuller, and we can both change and enlarge our mental pictures. Constantly we can extend, correct and deepen them: then we are behaving in a healthy way in our subjective world. But if we refuse to take in new mental pictures, or if we let the old ones grow rigid, we are unhealthy.

We find that the mental pictures are coloured by our feelings: our emotions are connected with them — hence we are so annoyed when 'OUR feelings are hurt!' The mental pictures are part of our personal life, which is permeated by feeling, and it is actually very hard to find a mental picture which is absolutely unconnected with feeling. Again, if we want to put the will to work, we need the mental picture of an aim before we can do so.

Once we have a picture of what this world of mental pictures is like, we can ask how it comes about and what connection the mental pictures have with reality. In *The Philosophy of Spiritual Activity* we are led to this by means of a number of steps, representing the views of various schools of philosophers, not stated for their own value but only as stages to be observed and then left behind by further advances. First we have the Naive Realist. This may be roughly defined as 'myself when I am too busy to think about what I am thinking about.' The Naive Realist just assumes that what he perceives is real, that his mental pictures are connected with the facts of reality. Most of us, in fact, are in this category most of the time, when we simply do something without questioning. We assume that our mental pictures are real, and act accordingly.

Once we start to ask questions, we may tend to become a Critical Idealist, who says: I move in my world of mental pictures, and use them, but how do I know that they actually correspond with an outer reality? When I see something outside, how do I know that the actual reality is like what I think I see?

Unless we reach this stage, we tend to remain shut up in the world of material things, to remain a materialist. The Critical Idealist attitude to life is the psychological experience which we can all reach — and then pass through, in order to escape from the world of mental pictures. He has had his world of mental pictures adjusted to the world outside, but now he should want to know whether his own soul-life is just his own, or whether it has any actual connection with the world outside. Does his personal world contain anything really real, or is he shut up behind blinkers? He looks at his mental pictures and asks: where is the element of reality?

Then he may, perhaps, think that the actual reality is, after all, in what is outside, but, if so, he still has to decide how much of this does not depend on his eyesight, his senses, his viewpoint. Thus, different people may see different things when both look at the same landscape from the same viewpoint, and we may ask whether the things which *we* do not see are really there at all. For example, a sheep may not really look as it appears to me, but what I see may depend on my seeing. There was a point where some philosophers, such as Kant, took even what we see as mere mental pictures, and denied the possibility of reaching the 'thing-in-itself.' If we accepted this, we should, as it were, be on the stage of a theatre, playing a part among stage scenery constructed by ourselves, and believing that the play, and the scenery, comprise the only reality.

But we can say: I have mental pictures, I know my subjective world, but what process did I go through in order to gain it? We then realize that all our mental pictures are the result of experience, past or present. And we may next ask: how does experience work? The percept comes from outside and the concept from inside, and where these meet the experience arises. If we see an oak tree, what we actually perceive is a number of details, but we do not 'perceive' the 'real oak tree,' for it is only when we have the concept that the details are all brought together and tell us that what we see *is* an oak-tree. We cannot say that the concept is our own personal thought and that the tree is outside: the concept is an essential part of the oak-tree, which *we* bring to meet the tree outside. For without the concept we should never build up the details perceived into an idea. The human consciousness has separated the tree outside from the concept, the 'archetypal idea of the tree, from which it takes its shape' and then brings the two together again to form the mental picture of the tree. We may compare how material is cut up and then sown together again to make clothes. In our 'knowing' we bring percept and concept together — and only human beings alone in the whole universe can do this. In other words, only human beings 'think.'

In the gap between the percept and the concept lies the whole world of mental pictures, and we could not have this unless we had first pulled the percept and the concept apart. We owe our subjective world, in which we become conscious of ourselves, to the fact that we have made a space between the percept and the concept. If there were no space, when we looked at the tree we should at once identify ourselves with it, but, having separated the percept and concept, we can form knowledge by bringing the two together again. This world of experience and mental pictures is constantly extending, because we constantly feed it with reality streaming in from both sides. Once we ask where the mental picture comes from, we see that it is the result of bringing something in from outside the subjective world. The percept is only a part of reality until the concept comes to meet it: when the two meet we are in touch with reality, and we have the chance of attaining to reality — or to error.

Our ultimate contact with reality is through thinking. We are aware of feelings but do not see where they come from: we only see the part of them within ourselves, and have made this personal before we become aware of it. We may liken sympathy with the fluid nature of water, which 'flows to meet' some person or thing, and antipathy with rocks, which interpose a solid, jagged barrier: if we visualize the beating on the rocks of the shore this can be taken as similar to the meeting of sympathy and antipathy. When we see ourselves liking or disliking something, we see a great cosmic force which has become personalized. The feeling is what I have made of the cosmic force when it has entered me, in a form personal to myself. We may compare how we breathe in a certain quantity of air, make personal use of it, and then expel it again: unless we are above the average, the use we make of these forces of feeling is usually unworthy of the force we have used.

But in thinking we see something in ourselves which is yet so much bigger than ourselves that it can reach out into the world. What we produce may be a very much reduced version of 'reality,' but we can see our thinking reaching out beyond ourselves to the real ideas. My thinking is not enclosed in my world of mental pictures: it can reach out to the world of reality and grasp this reality, so that I am not restricted to my own little world, nor to the world of matter, as is the Naive Realist, nor to the purely dream-world of the Critical Idealist. But by the time that our thought has reached the mental-picture stage, error may have crept in, even though the thinking did, earlier, make contact with the real idea. The world of ideas is *not* personal: all of us can 'know' an oak-tree, even though every one of us would draw it differently. The modern artist, who 'wants to paint the idea' is really juggling with the concept, and what he puts into his picture is likely to be either something purely personal or else a conglomeration of unrelated percepts.

The attitude of the Critical Idealist is very widespread today, and is frequently carried to a point where people do not consider the facts at all, but deal only in the mental pictures which they think are the right ones. They thus give way to a kind of 'wishful thinking' and ignore real life. This is largely the result of Kant, whose philosophy has now become a kind of instinct in many people. We see this strongly displayed in modern 'planning,' where committees of 'experts' pontificate about how the world outside is to be run, while never troubling to inform themselves what the real world is like. This is an attitude into which we are liable to fall again and again, but we must realize that our mental pictures are connected with reality, and must be constantly altered to bring them more and more into line with reality. So that we must pass beyond the stage of being Critical Idealists.

The thinking capacity is the one activity in us of which we have a direct percept without any mental picture intervening. For we perceive it directly, and through this we have our contact with reality. This thinking capacity does take us outside our world of mental pictures to the spiritual realities which have brought about the world which we perceive as percept. But it depends on how we use the thinking capacity. This is still only like a seed, which is not yet being fully used. And we shall never make proper use of our thinking while we are blinded by our world of mental pictures, as though this was all we have to work with. We must not confuse our mental pictures with 'truth,' for we have brought them about ourselves, and we can always extend and re-form them, relying not on the existing mental pictures but on our own thinking.

We find it uncomfortable to change our mental pictures, but they are only useful when they are subject to change. Unless we get outside our world of mental pictures, we are living neither in heaven nor on earth, but in an unreal little world of our own. In order to attain to self-consciousness, we have to separate percept and concept: in order to live with God we have to bring them together again. By doing so, we become responsible individuals; by not doing so we remain no more than individuals.

15

Limits of Consciousness?

Let us start with the biggest hindrance in the way of an understanding of our thinking by asking a very primitive question: do you identify yourself with your consciousness? Do you call this consciousness 'I' or do you consider that there is a part of yourself beyond and outside this consciousness? We may know in theory that there is more to us than our everyday consciousness. However, in our ordinary behaviour we tend to say: I am what I think I am, that is, that the conscious part is everything. This was, and still is, the difficulty of many philosophers.

We may find ourselves using 'I' in many different senses, even, perhaps, in the course of a single letter! It may, for instance, be a purely formal 'I hope you are well;' in other things one part of us may say 'I' while another part does not. We do not, in fact, always say 'I' to even the whole of our consciousness, but only to a part of it. Thus, we may want to go out and do something important, but another part of us would rather remain sitting by the fire; so, if we say. 'I want to go out,' it is only one part expressing itself.

Though most people most of the time do identify the consciousness with the 'I,' we can sometimes clearly recognize that there are parts of us which are not conscious. We may feel depressed owing to indigestion: the depression is in the consciousness, but the underlying cause of the indigestion is unconscious, for if we had to manage our digestion consciously we should have a full-time job doing it, like cows. Or, some people are affected by events among the stars. We can discover, in fact, that the assumption that the consciousness is 'I' is inadequate, that we must be bigger than our consciousness, by asking: is this conscious personality the same person who was present in my last incarnation, and will it be present in my next? This is not so, for the present-day conscious personality was not there in the last incarnation: had it been there we should remember that incarnation. Actually, we should find it hard to recognize as ourselves what was there, because it was so different from the present-day personality. Our behaviour, feelings and thinking were quite different then. We have two impulses now, one to be like what we were before, the other to be the opposite, and this sometimes explains our apparently illogical behaviour. Thus, the respectable person of this incarnation may suddenly 'crack,' though perhaps the cause of this has no connection with the previous incarnation, and the former impulse suddenly breaks through the crack, resulting in something completely 'out of character.' For we all have 'forgotten memories' in us, so that we may, for instance, suddenly find that we like or dislike something of which we have had no previous experience.

If, then, we want to find the self which goes from incarnation to incarnation, we shall not find it in the conscious part. To think that my consciousness is 'I' is merely a piece of Naive Realism, but we often even expect others to accept us as we think we are, for it gives us a shock if they see something else in us. One of the bad after-effects of psychoanalysis often is that the person who has undergone it thinks he has seen himself so thoroughly that never again can he get a proper view of himself. Besides, the psychoanalyst only looks at what is below the consciousness, but ignores the part of us which is outside but above it, the spiritual part of us.

But this assumption that the consciousness is all of us is the basis of the whole difficulty in which the Critical Idealist (of which Kant is the great example) finds himself. He says, here is my consciousness, and out there is the world, but I can never know its reality. I don't know how I can ever know anything about anything! In effect he says, this is 'I' (in my consciousness), and there is the world, and these two never make contact. But when we realize that the consciousness is not the whole of my self, we get over the difficulty, for the rest of 'me' is part of the world, so far as the consciousness is concerned. Thus, the way out for the Critical Idealist is to realize that there is something else of 'me,' with which I must reckon.

It is quite true that there is a difference between the way in which I see things and the way they really are. It is the realization of this difference which makes the Critical Idealist say: the world is one thing, but my picture of it is something quite different. We do find that our own mental picture of, say, a tree, differs from someone else's: as a result, the Critical Idealist doubts whether he can be really sure what the tree is. The point we have to come to is, where does this difference come from? Then we can see that my drawing of the tree comes out of my own sphere of consciousness, and is not so big as the real tree. I have left a lot out. What I have is that part of my experience of the tree which I have been able to take in and make my own. Thus, in general, my consciousness is smaller than the real world, and is always subject to limitations.

Look at the way in which the human sense-organs work. The squid, for instance, has the most primitive eye known. It has a hollow in its skin, open to the water outside: at the back of this hollow are the optic nerves, but, in place of an eyeball, it has sea water, which comes and goes. We, on the other hand, have an eyeball, and the nerves come to the edge of the boundary behind, and then turn in like pothooks, so that the ends of the nerves are pointing away from the light that comes into the eye. We are looking at the 'reflection of the world from the back of the eye,' yet we see the world as though it were in front of us. This is much more complicated than the squid's eye. But though the squid has the whole world before him he is not 'conscious of seeing' as we are. The human sense-organs are so arranged as to produce not only sense-impressions but consciousness of what we perceive. We are creating, with our sense-organs, a little world of which we can be conscious, and we ignore whatever we cannot cope with. For the whole of the world would be too big for us. So we retire into our reduced sphere of consciousness. We are not even big enough to take in the whole of ourselves.

We must regard our sphere of consciousness as changeable: it can be extended, when we learn something new, or reduced, as when we train ourselves not to hear things which disturb our concentration. And this proves that 'I' am not identical with my consciousness. In the sphere of consciousness we work with mental pictures, and these arise as a result of our having percepts and concepts. The concept becomes a mental picture: it becomes individualized, more connected with me, more like me — but, in fact, the process is usually one which limits the original concept. The mental picture usually has some memory of a percept in it: it is possible to have a mental picture without a percept first, but it will not become really strong unless there is some element of percept in it. We may also definitely reject a percept which we do not like, and return to our original concept.

Though the mental picture is part of my individual life, the percept and the concept are not. This is what the Kantians could not see. But we can go outside our individual world, to contact the reality in the form of the percept and concept, from which we then can produce a new mental picture, a reduced version of the percept and the concept. In actual fact my capacity to think and perceive goes out to meet reality: however much this capacity may be limited by our particular circumstances, which may affect the accuracy of my perception (for instance, defective sight) or that of my grasping the concept correctly (for instance, tiredness), what we perceive really is what is out there. And in our perceiving we do fetch something from beyond the range of our present conscious world. The percept comes into this little world of mine from one side and the concept from the other. And I can meet the reality in

the world because I am already in this world with the part of
me which is outside the conscious part.

The mental picture now becomes connected with the feelings and is made our own. For we become intensely interested
in things about which we have feelings — and we are usually
quite uninterested in what does not come in touch with our
feelings. The fact that we like or dislike the percept is of no
importance whatever for the world, but it is very important for
us. And the same applies to the concept. But this importance
which they have when they reach my consciousness is only my
own personal affair: it has no effect outside me unless I do
something to make it so. The fact that I connect myself with
the mental picture makes it real to me, but not to anyone else.
We touch reality through our thinking, but we become interested in it through our feeling. Thus, however much we know
the importance of eating for our welfare, we only *eat* as a result
of a feeling of hunger — or perhaps from a sense of duty,
which is also a feeling. Our sense of the importance of the
world thus depends on our feelings. So, to me, it is intensely
important that I should connect my feelings with my percepts.
But we must realize that our feelings do not affect what happens in the world, and that it is no good expecting that the
world will run itself to suit our feelings. And the realization
that the importance of our feelings is for ourselves alone is one
of the great human difficulties.

There is only one way in which feeling can be of importance to the world: this is when we take the feeling away from
ourselves and 'offer it to the concept,' when the feeling is taken
out again into the world of ideas and does have an effect on the
world. The feeling would then pass away into the world of living ideas, and we should no longer have the benefit of it. The
idea itself would 'grow feeling.' Thus, if one thinks an objective idea, with enthusiasm, the idea itself may go out into the
world — for instance, the abolition of slavery. This arose from
the concept of the dignity of the human being. What brought
about the abolition of slavery was that enough people were

fired by the idea, and set about the task. This was not directly brought about by Wilberforce talking to people, but from the fire of his enthusiasm kindling others so that they set about the task together. If we do good because we enjoy doing it or because we expect to get some benefit from doing it, this may do material good in the world, but it is not giving our feelings to the idea: it is merely doing what is very important to ourselves. What we do must be offered and done selflessly, not merely to relieve our own feelings — still less merely to indulge them. If we offer our feelings, we do not get the satisfaction ourselves, but we 'give the ideal wings' and let it go to someone else. It changes our life, but we do not reap feelings back again.

Another Naive Realist assumption, then, which we have to get past, is that the feeling which makes a thing important for me also makes it important for the world: it does not. The reality which extends beyond the content of my little world comes to me through the thinking and feeling, and the part which comes into my consciousness is what I can take into my sphere of feeling and make important to myself. But I can always extend and make contact with what is beyond this sphere of my present consciousness: I can always stretch it. So a right human mind should be a place where the whole world could become individualized without becoming limited, if I could extend the sphere of feeling to include the whole world. For the thinking can always reach out to the reality which I have not yet made my own, and by means of it I can expand myself to 'be the world.' If this could be attained, selfhood would cease to be egotistical.

This limited sphere of myself has arisen by means of percepts and concepts, and I am constantly bringing in more. Thus I am in contact with reality, even though my mental pictures are not *true* to reality because I have limited them — and even though there is also the possibility of falsification in the process of making them my own. Error is a limited concept, not put in connection with what the whole concept ought to be. We must not confuse the concept which has been reduced to a mental picture with the whole big 'idea' which we contacted when forming the concept. The mental picture has arisen from a process of thinking which contacted an idea much bigger than I could bring back. Nevertheless, the process of consciousness which brings back an inadequate mental picture has actually contacted reality. Thus, though we have minds limited in consciousness, we are not limited spiritually. We need not be content with the set of mental pictures which we now have — for we can go further.

16

Percept and Concept

It is very important to realize what is meant by Chapter 6 of *The Philosophy of Spiritual Activity:* we are looking back on what has been gained and we are aware that we have climbed out of the materialism of these times and how we did it. In order to observe this, it is a good plan to look at the three elements, the percept, the concept and the mental picture and see that we have a good mental picture of what they are, for the materialism of modern times has in great part arisen from unclearness of what they are.

Suppose one goes outside and shivers in a cold wind. We feel the sensation of cold, the pressure of the wind; we see things in motion, and we hear the sound of the wind. All these separate, single experiences are part of the percept. But when one says: 'I feel a cold wind,' one has introduced a concept. The percepts are all separate, unrelated experiences until the concept comes to meet them, but it is wrong to say that we merely 'add the percepts together' to make the concept. We could not add them together at all if it were not for the concept, which does not come to us as a derivative from the percepts but from the other direction: when it does arise it enables us to add the percepts together. No amount of going out on the doorstep will tell us that we are shivering because of the cold wind unless we have a concept. Thus animals do not *have* concepts: they have concepts *built into* them in the form of instincts. Animals have, indeed, been described as 'incarnated fixed ideas.'

We get the mental picture as a result of the experience of

bringing the percept and the concept together: it is the result, the harvest of the process. But mental pictures are what we work with in our thoughts. Thus there is a kind of modern 'thinking' which consists simply in 'arranging mental pictures.'

The mental picture is what is left over, what has been connected with the feeling and made our own: it is the 'furniture of our inner life.' The concept incarnates itself in us as a mental picture. But the concept is usually reached as a kind of reaction to the percept. By the time that we have the mental picture as an end-product, both the percept and the concept have been greatly reduced, and have been attached to ourselves, as they were not originally. This is why some people are so unwilling to change their existing mental pictures 'because they like them.' When people have points of view, and talk about their 'thoughts,' they are usually referring to mental pictures. We should, however, note that a percept need not always be outside us, nor need it be physical.

'Thinking,' as the word is used in *The Philosophy of Spiritual Activity,* is the activity of forming concepts, not the arranging of existing mental pictures.

Many people have very great difficulty in grasping the process by which we obtain the concept, and thus they say that the concept is the result of the percept. But we have to realize that the thinking activity reaches up to the world of ideas and brings down a concept, then forms a mental picture from it — personalizing it in the process. A concept which has not become a mental picture often seems 'vague' or 'abstract': nevertheless, the concepts, the ideas of the world, are common to us all. The mental pictures are the highly individualized forms which these take on in *my* mind, and are conditioned by my whole background.

Many people, confusing the mental picture and the concept, assume that all thoughts are private and personalized. But there is a 'public' and a 'private' part of our thinking, the concept being common to us all, and the mental picture my own private affair, which must be handled carefully. There are also those who think that the concept is abstracted from the mental picture, as the result of all similar experiences. These people say that the concept is not the 'archetypal image' but a shadow of the reality outside.

When, for instance, we plant seeds, we have faith in the 'archetypal flowers,' which are not in the world at the time when we plant the seeds. What is on the packet is a mental picture of the archetypal plant as incarnated in the mind of the advertiser.

In ordinary life we are usually all Naive Realists. The Naive Realist of today has to live on the assumption that the concepts are shadows but that the percepts are real. This comes out of the old assumption that the concept arises out of the percept. What can be seen and weighed and measured is considered to be 'real.' Thus, the Naive Realist only accepts what appears in perceptual form: if, for instance, he wishes to think about God, he must find a perceptual aspect of God. He has no faith in a God he can *think,* but he can believe in a God who can appear in a burning bush or turn water into wine. He likes 'miracles,' as perceptual 'proofs.' His God must have something about him connected with his percepts. He is willing to have imagination, but does not believe in this. God, as an 'old man with a long white beard,' is acceptable to him, but not the God who moves behind the order of the stars. We are all, and have to be, Naive Realists for much of the time, but we need not be nothing more than this. It is Naive Realism which has landed us in materialism, because it accepts only what can be seen and 'proved.' We see this in many modern scientists.

The Naive Realist, who accepts only percepts as 'true,' is in a very difficult position, because what he accepts is just the part which disappears and is impermanent. He sees to the actual flower, which blooms and fades, but not the archetypal flower — yet when he plants seeds he is acting out of faith in this archetype, though he is not conscious of doing so.

Very few people have more than vague thoughts about a life after death, but many of them still act as though this life after death were real. So we are not really Naive Realists all the time, for there are times when we have to act as though concepts were real. We realize, also, that the percepts as such are single. Nothing will bring them together without the concept. We cannot live without bringing them together, and thus the Naive Realist, not accepting the concept, has to fill in the gap with a lot of imaginary percepts, and he becomes a Metaphysical Realist. Thus, he feels that a table is hard and sees it with a certain 'solid' form, but he says that, *really,* it consists of a structure of atoms with space between them. He has never directly perceived an atom, but he looks for reality in another layer of hypothetical percept behind what he does perceive. This is really the Kantian standpoint: Kantians have to deal in perceptual images, and so invent the 'thing-in-itself' as the 'reality behind what we see.' The difference between Kant and the modern scientist is that Kant says that we are cut off from the 'thing-in-itself' and can never get to it, whereas the scientist forms an increasingly detailed picture of 'what is behind,' in the form of the atomic structure, and so forth. Others would proceed by induction, by comparing all observed experiences of tables and taking what is common to all these as the qualities of the 'table-in-itself.' They do not accept that they can *know* the table-in-itself, but only certain qualities of it: we are still imprisoned in the circle of our percepts. But the Metaphysical Realist has to add something (which is not actually perceived) to the original percepts, whereas we ought to allow that the concept is real: then we shall find out that what is detail in the percept is a whole in the concept, which comes out of the world-whole.

But, in order to do this, we must cease to be Naive Realists, for we must admit that the percept is only completed when the concept comes to meet it, and that the concept is equally real, since it comes from the ultimate reality.

The Metaphysical Realist is a person who deals with the world by bringing in extra, hypothetical percepts, whereas the Critical Realist starts by looking in his own mind. But the two are really very similar at heart. People have more faith in Metaphysical Realism, because the hypotheses are presented in perceptual form, however imaginary these added percepts are. We may, for instance, note how much more faith people have in flying saucers than in the life after death, and even have the need to man their space-craft with creatures similar to human beings! Naive Realism allows people to believe a great deal which can be believed without thought, just because it is presented convincingly. On the other hand, the truly real world is that of the ideas, the world of the concept and not that of the percept.

Not only do we reach reality by bringing the percept and the concept together, but it is we who have pulled them apart in the first place. The very thought 'here am I and there is the world' is a concept which we must form as we learn to speak and think. A very young baby is one with the world, and does not speak or think. But when we take the two apart and then bring them together again we leave a space between for our own little personal world of mental pictures. If we did not have this space we would live like the animals. Having made this space, we must fill it with our 'little world in the great world,' by bringing percepts and concepts together. But now error has come in, for this personal world is always less than the 'great world,' though we can always enlarge it and make it nearer to this. Our mental pictures are a reduced copy of reality. When we are asleep, we cease to separate percept and concept; the whole 'great world' rushes in on us, and we cannot cope with it, so we lose consciousness. Difficulty in falling asleep is often due to unwillingness to let go of our own private world. What makes us human beings is the fact that we do make this world of our own minds, which should become a reflection of the whole world. It is the task of the human mind continually to take in new and greater ideas, constantly to expand by using our powers of perceiving and of conceiving to bring more into our own world. Although the mind is limited at any given time, it is not limited forever. Thinking and perceiving beyond the present sphere of mental pictures brings new reality into my personal world. There are very few people who cannot think, but very many who will not. There are limits to my present knowledge, but there are no frontiers to knowledge as such.

The reality is the concept: the name we give to the thing is merely incidental. The ultimate fact is that *I* have brought about the division between percept and concept, and that I must bring them together again. The percept has the form which it has because of me, and I can only overcome its limitations by bringing to meet it the concept from the world of ideas. The percept is only the part of reality which I can perceive, and I must 'put it right' by adding the concept to it. The real world must work in me, and does so through my thinking.

The Relationship of Thinking to Feeling and Will

The first part of Chapter 8 of *The Philosophy of Spiritual Activity* is a recapitulation of the first half of the book, but from another point of view. This briefly is, 'I am a human being. The world around me is full of many things, and one of these things is "I." But when I look into myself as one of the things of the world I find in myself a power of making sense of all these things through the power of thinking. This enables me to see myself as subject and the rest as objects. The rest is "given," but the thinking activity is not, for I produce it myself.'

This is the position we have won as a result of the first half of Steiner's book. The rest of this chapter tells what happens to those who find feeling or willing more real than thinking, who consider thoughts cold, abstract things but regard a strong reaction of feeling as 'real,' or who say that reality consists in 'things happening outside,' whether I have myself had a hand in causing this or whether I merely observe it; in other words, that it is the will which leads us to reality. But we have to discover that our thinking is our real connection with reality, and we can only see this by first looking at and then overcoming the illusions in the other two views.

The people who believe in feeling may not *like* the feelings which they have, but they will consider that even hate or fear are more real than 'just passing them by.' They judge everything by the feeling-reaction brought about in themselves. But feeling is the quality which makes a thing 'interesting to me': it is essentially a personal thing. We see, for instance, that it is easier to eat something which we dislike than something which is merely flavourless and boring. It is very difficult to take in anything for which we have no feeling of any kind — but our lack of feeling has nothing to do with the reality of the thing outside. These people, however, consider that their personal feelings should be extended over the whole world: if they are not interested in something, then that is the end of it!

If they carry this 'Philosophy of Feeling' further, they become Mystics. They seek immediately to experience what must be known, trying to elevate feeling, which is a purely individual activity, into a universal principle. They would base even the world-reality on the feeling which it produces in themselves. They look on the true spiritual life as a great emptiness, full of feeling. They wish to put feeling in the place of knowledge, to feel reality instead of trying to grasp its essence. We cannot, of course, do without feeling, but it should be kept in its proper place.

Those who think that the will is the reality tend to become materialists, because what interests them is what can be made to happen among the things of the world. 'Real life,' to them, is when something is being done or made, as in a factory. They say to themselves: when I use my will, I cause the situation around me to change, instead of merely receiving the impact of the outer world, and I see similar forces of will causing the events of nature outside myself. When I change the situation, they say, I am really living: what is happening there is the activity of will-force, which is real and fundamental, whereas thinking and feeling are only secondary. However, they can experience the will inside themselves, but they cannot know that a will-force is operating in outer events unless they use their thinking first. They think of this outer will, and then discount the thinking. Thus, the materialist tends to put will where thinking ought to be.

We can now go on to the relationship between thinking and willing. But first we must look at the nature of thinking, as here described, for the main difficulty is that we usually pay attention only to the old thoughts which are the result of previous thinking, and confuse these with the thinking activity itself. The darkness of the shadow of the dying thoughts is in proportion to the brightness of the activity of thinking, and we are apt to judge our thinking by the darkness of the shadow.

Let us try to imagine a pear-tree in full blossom against the blue sky. If it were April, we could go out and look at the real tree, and it is clear that we should get more 'reality' from the actual tree than from our mental picture of it, which would seem dry and lifeless by comparison. In the presence of the real pear-tree, we could have deep feelings: we might feel the urge of our will-forces to break off a spray of blossom to take away with us, so as to unite ourselves in this way with the tree. We could also, instead of merely thinking *about* the tree, instead of being satisfied with mere feelings about it, or with taking a piece of it home, want to think our way into the nature of the tree, to 'think the tree,' and, if we succeed in doing this, we may come through to a feeling which is not personal but is actually the 'cosmic feeling' about the tree, even to the activity of the cosmic will in the tree. Then we find our thinking opening up into feeling and willing, but on a new level. The thought-picture, then, will have come out of a living experience. Those who say that by following thinking they are going away from the 'warm reality' do not know what they are talking about, for if they followed their thinking properly they would reach a deeper level of feeling.

This form of extended thinking is what allows us to know things beyond what the physical senses perceive, for it can be extended to supersensible beings. If we are thinking wrongly, the thought will fade away: if we are thinking rightly, it will grow stronger, giving us our own test for truth. This capacity is present in us all as a seed, because the Holy Spirit was given to humankind at Pentecost. But it has taken a long time for this gift to become a capacity, and this is why, in early times, people had, as it were, 'conversations with the Holy Spirit,' as with something outside themselves. And many people today wait for something to be given to them from outside, whereas we should use this new kind of thinking to obtain reality for ourselves. Thus, present-day scientists have all the percepts lined up, but do not believe that they have the power to add anything to these.

We no longer just have to believe something because some 'authority' has told it to us, but we can think our way into it and realize for ourselves whether it is true or not. We must find confidence in the capacity which we all have, with which we can to grasp spiritual reality through our own thinking — and then we must put this capacity to use. We have already overcome any idea that the thinking is derived from the percept: we must see it as a spiritual activity: when we use it in this way, we are having a spiritual experience of a purely spiritual content.

When we have once grasped this, we read that the bodily organism is, in fact, neither the instrument nor the means by which the thinking activity takes place, but it does give the opportunity for it to be exercised. For it pushes out the existing activity of the brain and acts on it instead, leaving marks on it as our feet do when we walk over soft ground. We find the consciousness of ourselves where the two meet: the ego-force is in the thinking activity but the ego-consciousness is built upon the human bodily organization, being 'reflected back' from the body. Where the self really is, we are not conscious of it. Thinking takes place *on,* not in, the bodily organization, and actually has a destructive effect on it.

We have now to find the connection between the will and the thinking. The process of consciousness which is used when we follow such an experience as that of the tree is not only used for external objects which we can see or perceive with the senses: the same process can be used to apply to entirely inner experiences. Then the percept is usually a mental picture, and the concept comes from the world ideas to meet this, the whole process happening within ourselves.

An idea which we have once thought enters the world of mental pictures and can then become a percept. The higher kind of thinking can enable us to grasp in knowledge realities which never show themselves to our sense-perception in the world outside. A good example of this is thoughts of pure mathematics.

Rudolf Steiner brought down many realities of the spiritual world from the sphere of ideas into the sphere of mental pictures through his own conscious activity. In his books and lectures he offers us mental pictures which we can then perceive as percepts. He was such a master in this sphere of consciousness that he could bring us mental pictures which are true representations of the ideas from which they came. Most others using this process cannot do it so well, and their experiences are likely to be less accurate. But this is a question of degree, not of process. When we use Rudolf Steiner's mental pictures as percepts, we can in fact reach up with our thinking activity to the ideas from which he brought them down, and thus we are able, in fact, to know these realities and not just believe in them because he said so. Those who say that they 'know' the reality of, for example, angels or the life after death or reincarnation can do so honestly if they have fulfilled this process of consciousness. But if they do not think the idea themselves, they are merely believing in the same way as do those who believe what the Pope says. Rudolf Steiner wrote *The Philosophy of Spiritual Activity* before any of his other works, so that he offered people the knowledge of this process of consciousness before giving them the insights from the spiritual world.

People who really grasp a spiritual thought or fact have in reality used this process to do so, but it happens very quickly (being, really, outside earthly time) so that we seldom notice what we have been doing, and therefore most spiritually-minded people have already used this kind of thinking without having any deliberate intention of doing so. It can happen in a flash. But there is a tremendous value in being aware of the process and of how it works, so as to be able to use it at will and not have to wait for the flash of inspiration to come of itself. This kind of thinking brings a purely spiritual experience of purely spiritual content.

This means that the bodily organization has not in any sense produced this process. But the thinking activity makes contact with the bodily organization, which then becomes a mirror throwing back the thought into consciousness. The reality of the ego is present in the activity of thinking: the consciousness of the ego is brought about by the contact of the thinking with the bodily organization. But once this has been brought about it enters the world of thought and continues to live there as a thought even after the contact with the bodily organization has ceased.

This comes about as a result of a principle which works all through the human being: where the reality is, the consciousness is not, and where the consciousness is, the reality is not. Reality is in the thinking, consciousness in the thought. Parallel to this can be seen, in the physiological sphere, that we are aware of our self-consciousness in the head-and-nerve organization, whereas we have the reality of it in the blood and the metabolic system. The thinking activity enters the bodily organization through the brain and nervous system, throws out the life-process and substitutes its own process, thereby spreading consciousness and the forces of death. But this allows us to be conscious, while we are living in the body, of purely spiritual experiences of purely spiritual content.

The ideas enter the human ego, the self, through this higher thinking, and, passing through the 'crossing point of the lemniscate,' can pass out into the earthly world through the actions of the self. This is the means by which new spiritual impulses are incarnated into the earthly world, and this incarnation can continue. It passes through the 'crossing-point' of the self, the human ego.

18

The Moral Idea and Moral Activity

We have dealt with the creative kind of thinking which reaches up to the world of ideas, which have to be brought down by the self and pass over by means of the will into action. Though the world of ideas are above us and in the spiritual world, action can only be brought about by the individual. Thinking, in its own character, contains the real 'I' but does not contain the 'ego-consciousness,' which is present in the impact of the thinking on the physical organism. The ego, or self, is thus the crossing-point between thinking and will.

When we have reached the point of seeing where the self stands between thinking and will, we must next ask what is the relationship between the ego and action. We can now say: an action has a double source, in two things which have to come together: the motive and the 'spring of action.' The motive is a factor of the nature of a concept or a mental picture; the spring of action is a factor in the will resulting directly from the disposition or character of the individual. We may all have a motive in common, but we may yet all react differently to it, because it does not necessarily touch off the same spring of action in the same way. This may also be the same for all the people in one place, as in the case of a fire. The motive is the momentary determining cause of an act of will, but the spring of action is the permanent determining factor in the individual, largely connected with the personal nature, conditioned by predisposition, character and 'make-up' and brought about by various aspects of the personality, such as upbringing, environment, heredity, nationality, and, generally, by the individual's world of mental pictures which, itself, is the result of all his previous experiences, whether 'digested' or not. The 'undigested' experiences will have an effect different from that of the 'digested' ones, but all are present and have an effect on the spring of action.

Many people perform a large proportion of their actions either as a result of such previous experiences, because that was how their parents behaved, or for similar reasons. But part of our predisposition consists of the concepts which we are used to forming, and the mental pictures which are the results of our thinking and experience. There is, however, a point at which one can become so enthusiastic for an idea that the predisposition can be overcome. The spring of action then becomes the idea itself, acting directly.

The motive always lies in the sphere of mental pictures, though this is not always so easy to see. Say that we like ice-cream, and on a hot day hear the bell of the ice-cream van: the spring of action is our liking for ice-cream and the fact that we are the kind of person who is accustomed to go and get what he wants. But the motive cannot be a feeling of pleasure — for this will not fully occur until we have got the ice-cream: it is the mental picture of the ice-cream we have previously enjoyed and the thought of the future pleasure. To a certain extent, we may 'astrally' experience the pleasure of the ice-cream even before we start to eat it, by a process of the astral body extending outside the physical and making contact with it, but, in human beings, the main reaction is through mental pictures. In the case of an animal, which has a pattern of behaviour, but not mental pictures in the human sense, the astral can be much more extended and there may be a large measure of direct contact with the external object, as when a hawk is able to swoop straight on to a distant mouse or a vulture 'happens to arrive' where there is a fresh corpse.

Even though a human motive may start as a feeling, it must, generally, turn into a mental picture before it can result in an action. Advertising depends on putting in front of people a mental picture which the advertiser hopes will release the spring of action and make others buy the article. The mental picture is supplied in a very attractive form, which the advertiser hopes will act on the greatest number of people. Political propaganda, however, seldom troubles even to provide a good mental picture (apart from glorious promises) but depends on innumerable repetitions, ramming a motive into people so hard and so often that the predisposition tends to be overcome and the spring of action directly struck.

Though the motive is always in the sphere of mental pictures, it can come about in many ways and at many levels. It may be connected with the content of the situation, or the mental picture may appeal either to one's egotism or to one's altruism. Some people will turn every situation to their own advantage somehow: others seek that content of a situation which provides for the good or benefit of others or of humankind in general, or the concept of the greatest possible good to everyone by means of some particular idea. Or the moral value of the motive may be the important thing to them, perhaps because it has been erected into a moral law as a result of the thinking of others (as in the case of the Ten Commandments). There are many, today, with the concept of such 'fixed laws of ethics' or 'universal laws of God,' which they consider must be enforced by justice, irrespective of actual human laws. An excellent example of this was seen in the Nuremburg trials, with the concept of 'crimes against humanity' unknown to any national code of law. This idea of 'universal law' provides a moral motive for many people today.

A stage further, ethically, is when one listens, not to an outside law, but to the inner voice of conscience, whose commands provide the motive. The motive is then decided by a principle, not by law: motives are decided by the content of the action, judged by the principle, for instance, kindness or the 'done thing.'

But it is possible to go beyond this, when intuitive thinking can reach up to the moral idea itself, and bring this down to meet the content of the situation. This is the morally best action, because it is the only really free one: it goes beyond principle. At this level of morality, the spring of action and the motive coincide: the action depends neither on the predisposition nor on authority, but depends only on the ideal content.

Kant said: I should so act that my action is a pattern for all others. But this is not a free action, for the motive should be individual, implicit in one, unique situation and not to be exactly repeated. From this Kantian idea springs the conception of the absolute 'right thing to do,' the 'only possible answer' determined by the content of the situation. The Kantian would act out of duty, on principle, saying: I never do such a thing, or, I always act in this way.

We must not, however, simply throw our fixed principles overboard: we must hold to them until we can replace them by something better. All the same, we can see around us what a lot of harm is done by people with most excellent motives trying to lay down 'universal principles,' which they say should hold good for everyone. Even if I establish, out of my own conscience a principle which I then consider to be universally valid for myself, I am turning my mental pictures into tablets of stone: I have used my conscience once and then made a rule out of what I have once found. This is still not the highest form of action, for so long as I am acting on a fixed principle I am not free, because the principle itself is binding me. Such principles may be very heroic, but they can also have disastrous results, whether because they are too rigid or because they are mistaken.

If we get beyond this stage, we put moral activity in the place of principle. We accept the fact that every situation is different, that our thinking has the power to reach up to the idea, which is full of God's morality, and to bring down a completely new moral spring of action into the situation. This may produce the same result as the mere application of a principle, but it is decided, not by the immediate content of the situation, but by the moral idea which has been touched by the moral intuition exercised by the ego. Actions of this kind may be very small, but, even here, the action really should be decided by the individual situation.

Principles, however, are more easily understood than are moral intuitions. To produce an example of the latter, one would have to tell a long story of a complete situation, out of which an entirely individual action has arisen. It is impossible to give an example of a future moral intuition.

The consequence of the moral intuition is that the action springs from a moral activity which has to be set in motion every time — and this makes life rather hard today. It is also very difficult to see how one can tell anyone else what to do — though it is possible to offer him a mental picture which may enable him to reach up to a moral intuition. The amount of the moral idea which an individual can bring down will vary from one time to another, and so will the state of the mental picture which can be formed as a result, so that the answer obtained will differ accordingly. Rudolf Steiner once said that it was very painful to him to see how people who could have worked together for high spiritual purposes would sometimes take a dislike to each other for quite trivial reasons. But his intuition was so much greater that he could see the possibilities which they were ignoring.

19

Freedom and Morality

We have now to proceed with the question of what a free decision is. In *The Philosophy of Spiritual Activity* we are first given the general idea, and only then are we told how it works out practically. We had arrived at the position of one who finds freedom as contrasted with the position taken up by Kant: 'So act that the principle on which you act can apply equally to everyone else.' This leads to bondage to our own principles and loses sight of the fact that only the individual can create a free action. Kant is the originator of the idea, so beloved by present-day people, of the 'right thing' of universal application, which I have only to discover and carry out, which would also be right for everyone else. For it would be the 'moral law' which I should have to discover and then follow, something already existing and outside myself.

To arrive at an action, we need a motive and a spring of action. To reach a free spring of action, we must overcome our predisposition to a point where an intuitively-grasped idea itself becomes the spring of action. Thus, this kind of freedom depends on an inner moral achievement, which does not depend on outside circumstances, nor yet on what someone else has done before. It depends on overcoming our own nature, until we are able to act independently of any compulsion arising from our own predisposition. Such compulsions can take many forms, such as 'knowing our place,' or 'expecting to receive what we have been accustomed to' or 'insisting on our rights': people who are bound by these can seldom rise to any action of real human or spiritual value, because they are bound by their predisposition.

To arrive at a free motive (which lies in the sphere of mental pictures), we must overcome our old thoughts and find a motive arising out of the new, higher kind of thinking. But this, like the free spring of action, is a free, intuitive idea, and we then find that the motive and the spring of action have become the same thing, both being arrived at by intuitive thinking — though they differ at all the lower levels.

What moves one to such an action is enthusiastic devotion for the idea itself — acting 'out of love' (though this has no sentimental implication), whereas Kant would act from duty. Where we get into difficulties in practice is to distinguish between the two, which may look the same in the result: it was how the result was reached which matters. For principles are, essentially, either one's own or someone else's previous intuitive thinking, as one might say 'bottled or canned,' whereas a free action is the 'fresh' article, a new intuitive idea created for the occasion. And the canned idea may not be properly applied in circumstances which may have changed since it was fresh. Intuitive thinking does not exclude principles: it merely lifts them to a higher level and recreates them.

We do not make a decision in the abstract: we usually wait for the situation to arise and then consider what to do: the decision, then, refers to a particular and unique set of circumstances. Those who work on intuitive thinking treat the situation as a matter of knowledge, and then reach up to the moral idea and let this show what the decision is to be. This sphere of ideas is one in which morality is present, so the moral impulse is a natural part of the idea, whereas morality is not naturally present in nature unless human beings bring it in. Animals do not experience morality, but do live in a world of wisdom. Goodness has continually to be born into the world through human beings: only thus is life brought into the world. So we can see how very important it is not to derive the moral idea merely out of the situation, by applying a fixed principle. The moral content is in the idea, which *we* have to bring into the situation.

If one finds a wallet containing money and takes it to the police, one may merely act on principle, because one is honest. But if one starts from the actual circumstances and then considers 'what do I do in these circumstances,' one will probably arrive at the same kind of action, but by a method which will have forwarded the aims of Christ. If, further, someone comes up claims that the wallet is his, the man of principle might still insist that he must take it to the police as the other may not be telling the truth, but intuitive thinking may tell the finder that this person is honest and entitled to be given the wallet. This need not take any appreciable time, as most people imagine. Such examples are very difficult to describe, especially in theory, for every case is individual and can only be described after the event: such examples will therefore always sound very 'theoretical' to other people.

When one decides on principle, one usually is brought to a decision 'either — or': when using intuitive thinking, there is seldom such a direct dilemma, and a third course may appear. The one who acts on principle may be content merely to follow the principle, without going any further. In the case of the wallet, his first thought would probably be how to discharge his responsibility by handing it over to someone else, whereas the one acts on intuitive thinking would probably bring into the situation some constructive thinking which would not be there without his effort, including, perhaps, practical attempts to find the owner — not just handing it over and getting rid of it. A free action is done through creative activity, whereas the action done from principle is automatic and uncreative. To consider what is to be done, in detail, in the particular circumstances, to 'think the idea' (not 'think about' it), is morally higher.

Out of this we find that what allows us to make enough connection with the idea to make us want to do something is enthusiasm, love for the idea, realization that this idea ought to be incarnated into the world. But, as this kind of thinking can only happen in individual human beings, some would say that the result would be anarchy. But true individuality which contacts the idea is itself connected with the moral sphere of the world, whereas our criminal or evil acts come from our 'common human nature' which is not the same thing. For the part of us which contacts the idea cannot have love for what is not moral. What we do 'wrong' is part of what we have in common, but our true individuality is what sets us free from this.

If we reckon that the impulse is of the same value as the action (as stated in the Sermon on the Mount), we see that all of us have the impulses in us, only most of us do not bring them to incarnation as actions. It is our 'common human nature' which brings about our unfree actions.

The objection is also raised that this is describing ideal human beings and not people as they are. But we can make ourselves more like this, and we should make it our aim to draw nearer to the ideal set before us. We must have faith in our power to attain freedom, in order to carry human evolution a stage further in accordance with the purpose of Christ.

We may ask: if intuitive thinking means that the thought arises through an individual and is carried over into action by him, where is the common part? We all start with the same sphere of moral ideas, just as people of principle have their principles in common. But the fact of having principles in common tends to cause dissension, because it tends to make us think that others should all be like us — or, if they are not, should be made to conform. In the new way, the freedom of the individual leads to community between individuals: because we recognize that the others have reached up to the same sphere of ideas, we can live in harmony with them, even though the result has been different owing to the different way in which part of the content of the idea has been brought down, even though we may not at all agree that what they have done is 'right.' No individual is big enough to grasp the whole idea and incarnate it, but we may recognize in someone else a part of it which we were unable to grasp. Community does not mean uniformity. But we find it hard to contact the individuality of others, because they obtrude their 'personality' in front of it. Where we enter the sphere of the true individuality, we reach something essentially selfless, which can have harmony with others in spite of differences, whereas personalities can only agree when there is uniformity.

The final stage reached in Chapter 9 of *The Philosophy of Spiritual Activity* is a description of what will grow out of freedom in the evolution of the future, when one part of the human being moulds another part. I bring to meet the percept outside me something which was not in it, but there is one place where the act of bringing percept and concept together is an act of will, not of knowledge. This is in my relations with myself as a human being, where, by bringing the concept into the percept, I can alter the percept (that is, myself as I am) for the better. Nature and society have evolved the human being to a certain point, but the human being must do the rest for himself, making freedom a creative inner activity, to alter and improve the percept of ourselves, which we realize is not up to the level of the concept of what a human being ought to be.

The clue is to realize where the true individuality lies and how the intuitive thinking takes place, while realizing how difficult it is to build up examples. But most of us can look back on our own lives and realize when we have exercised this kind of thinking: by learning to recognize it, we may become more able to exercise it at will, without waiting for the 'inspiration.' Morality should become a living thing in us, not a mere 'standard' existing outside. We can perhaps see intuitive thinking best in unexpected acts of kindness, not those carried out 'philanthropically.' This kind of intuitive thinking is closely allied to common sense, but common sense raised to a higher level: nevertheless, common sense should be a good starting-point. Thus, it should be more easily within reach of the English-speaking people, who so often have a good basis of common sense from which to start.

Creating the Vessel for the Holy Spirit

We have seen that there is a naturally-ordained community among human beings, arising from the fact that, though we can neither think nor act for others but must do so individually, we are not cut off from them as a result of this. For the sphere of ideas is common to us all, so that, if we can reach it, we are all making contact with the same thing. This brings us together, though we have to go through the process of consciousness individually.

In practice, however, this community which ought to arise is very often not attained. The sense that the world of ideas is common to all is missed when the process is not properly completed, and it is thus very difficult to attain to the community. Many of us tend to have our own 'private worlds' which represent for us our spiritual life, and to which others, except perhaps a chosen few, have no access. But this is in itself a contradiction of the position we have reached, for we ought to be able to share this private world. Actually, we can only share the world of ideas as one free person with another, but not if either is locked up in his own disposition or personality. If, on principle, we can see that the sphere of ideas is common to all, we still have to find it in freedom, or else we merely get our own, personal picture of it, which we can only share with someone who has gained a similar picture. The approach to the idea must also be sincere, and the process must be carried to a point where the other can share it. It is possible to bring the idea merely into the sphere of one's own personal experience, but not to a point where the other can see through the words to the idea itself. One must not try to take something from the sphere of one's own mental pictures and push it into the other's mind, but should try to express the thing in such a way that others, using the words as a percept, can themselves reach the same idea and see for themselves that the words are correct. They may receive quite a different mental picture, but this will probably serve to correct and amplify one's own, and thus bring something new into the world.

This is what Rudolf Steiner was so often able to do in his lectures, enabling his hearers to 'think the idea' for themselves and so attain to something new. The qualities of the consciousness soul make it more possible to reach the 'it thinks in me,' passing beyond the 'I think' of the intellectual soul. We should not 'try to make the thoughts our own,' but should let them live in us. What matters is that we touch the point which will enable the other to reach the origin of it all: the less of one's own personality that enters into it, the better. Many a modern 'good orator' does not make contact with the idea at all, but is merely appealing to what he hopes will be the personal feelings of his hearers.

Generally speaking, unfreedom in spiritual matters comes about when the process is incomplete and one person is trying to thrust his own views on to others: he then often puts a lot of will into his speaking, using the will which should have been used to complete the process of consciousness in trying to thrust his own opinion on to the other. We nearly always find that when this happens he has not completed his thought-process: when this happens, there may be a tendency towards gesticulation and other outward signs of emotion, even anger. Thus we see that a process of consciousness is necessary before we are in a position to share an idea with others. If we do not complete this process, we may become convinced that our own private spiritual world is the only right one, which must be propagated and defended. The people who can and do complete the process must learn to be very patient with the others, for their mental pictures will not complete his but will be merely personal ones: this may give rise to bitter divisions. We see an example of this in the multitude of bitterly hostile religious sects in the sixteenth century, at a time when it was not yet possible for most people to complete the process.

Chapter 9 of *The Philosophy of Spiritual Activity* ends with the point that the process of consciousness which leads to freedom is that by which we attain to full humanity, a process which nature and society have carried to a certain point but which we still have to complete by our own efforts. Chapter 10 deals with the way in which people receive the moral impulses for their actions, starting with the Naive Realist person, and then showing, step by step, how we can climb out of this to Metaphysical Realism and finally to the position of a free human being, a true human being.

What we attained before was reached by a process of thought: now we go through a process of development in experience. A healthy person goes through these stages as he grows up, and will therefore have experienced them all at some time in his life. For, as small children, we are all Naive Realists. We are continually in the process of trying to attain freedom, never in a static position of 'having attained it,' and we all have the tendency, however far we have climbed, to fall back, temporarily, into the earlier stages again. We cannot expect to 'attain freedom once and for all.'

The Naive Realist regards nothing but his percepts — what he can see and feel and touch — as 'real.' He therefore expects to find completely perceptible motives for his actions. In this stage, therefore, he would like to find some person whom he sees as greater than himself, whether by virtue of position in society or as a result of confidence in him, to tell him what to do, so that he can follow this 'good example.' The source of the motive is a 'perceptible' other person — as is rightly the case with small children, who should be led by an authority of this kind.

Then the Naive Realist may advance to the stage where he no longer follows the authority of one person, but begins to look for the 'example' in a group, such as the law, or a religious body, or the government, or his racial group. This, however, is still something 'perceptible,' still 'bigger than himself,' though he may now have come to the conclusion that he is quite as well able to think as any other individual.

Then he may realize that even this group is made up of people 'no bigger than himself,' when he may turn to God, as a being much greater than, yet separate from, himself, but usually expressed in perceptible terms, as when he appears in a burning bush, or is represented as an old man in the sky, with a fatherly mind. This is the kind of mental picture of God which the Naive Realist reaches when he looks for an authority not 'visible' in the crudest sense, yet still in a certain sense 'perceptible.' This is the position of those who regard the will of God as a definitely thought-out plan, outside ourselves, something analogous with our own plans but bigger, something which we are bound to carry out. This also the way in which the God of the Old Testament is represented, or the Lord of Don Camillo.

It is now possible to reach a higher development, when the Naive Realist begins to accept moral impulses which maintain themselves in his consciousness as principles, independently of God. These principles originally came from him, but have now come to attain to a sort of 'perceptibility' of their own. An example is the 'idea of honesty,' against which we can measure our own actions, almost as with a moral thermometer. The principle remains a 'perceptible object,' but these standards are already not quite so 'perceptible' as before, and the person has become a 'metaphysical realist,' who cannot explain his percepts out of themselves but assumes a further layer of percepts behind these, by which he hopes to explain them, although these other assumed percepts are not actually perceived. When we reach this stage, we are assuming something behind the perceptible world which we do not perceive: these principles depend on a 'moral order of the world,' which we do not perceive but merely accept.

This type of Metaphysical Realism has attained a great power in our times, for the Nuremberg trials were based on it, assuming a kind of 'divine law of God' which all people are bound to follow, though there was no actual law to justify what was done. It is assumed that God has ordained some 'standard of decency,' which we therefore observe, or at least which we use as a yardstick by which to measure our own actions. (But, of course, the individual frequently assumes that he, and only he, has a correct picture of this divine ordinance, to which others must be made to conform).

The Metaphysical Realist, in a further extension of his nature, sees the moral acts of men as fulfilling the purposes of a God outside, an absolute spiritual being hidden behind all phenomena. He regards the moral principles which his reason contains as a manifestation of this being. Moral laws, according to him, are dictated by the absolute, and man's task is to discover, by means of his reason, what these laws are, and carry them out. Man has become the slave of the absolute will. Freedom is denied.

To climb out of this and reach the sphere of freedom, we must realize that these principles and standards — which do exist and in many cases ought to exist — have originated in the thoughts of individual human beings, not in a mysterious 'moral order' which no one has ever seen. It is only that they have got divorced from human thinking and now have taken on an independent existence. The moral impulses, which do come from God, reach the earth through the medium of human thinking. I am therefore, personally, connected with a real being in an actual, individual process. It is not necessary to suppose that a human being, in order to be good, must blindly obey something outside himself: he can reach up to the idea and, out of his own thinking, form his own will, which is yet (if the process is rightly carried out) in tune with the will of God. This is in contrast with the law of Moses, formulated at a time when Metaphysical Realism was still the highest stage possible.

Even the voice of conscience is only expressing thoughts: it is not something outside myself but is a part of me, so that I and my conscience are creating something together. The human being who can reach up from Metaphysical Realism to freedom is making himself fully human and completing his destiny. For this is the intention of the working of the Holy Spirit, and the human being who fulfils himself will become a vessel suitable for the Holy Spirit to use. But the Holy Spirit will only come to me as a result of my own free moral impulse, not as an outside process. The Holy Spirit is tending to become the spirit of man, so that in later times he should be represented not as a dove but in human form. But he can only become 'human' insofar as we enable him to do so.

Moral Technique

Suppose that on a warm spring afternoon, when the golden crocuses have opened, we see a bee on its way to a crocus, and a child asks us what the bee is doing, and why, what are we to say? According to Naive Realism, most of us would tend to give a description of the bee's sequence of actions, gathering honey, returning to the hive to store it, etc., with an implied chain of purposes and motives similar to our own. But this is what really cannot be said about the bee. If I go out shopping to buy certain things, I have a mental picture of these things which I want, and I go out with a motive, a purpose, but we cannot say this about the bee. With the human being, there must be a bringing together of percept and concept, which then produce a mental picture: there must be a motive existing in the sphere of mental pictures. But to speak of the bee in this way is to make a quite unjustified analogy with human actions. The bee does not separate percept and concept, and therefore cannot have a mental picture in the human sense. It is only in the case of human beings and their actions that we can speak of 'means serving ends,' or even, really, of 'cause and effect.' For, though one action may follow another in time, though one may actually be the direct result of the other, the two percepts would merely stand side by side in a mind unable to connect them, by means of the corresponding concepts, in a 'cause-and-effect' relationship.

There are innumerable books about nature based on this analogy, assuming that all other creatures have mental processes similar to ours, that they reason, even that they are moved by moral considerations. By an extension of this assumption, we are easily led to assume that God's mind, also, works in a human way, that he has a 'thought-out world-plan,' into which we must all fit. They assume that God has a consciousness like ours, that he forms a mental picture as we do, and then 'plans' like a kind of 'super-government,' even that heaven is a kind of 'super welfare state.' As part of the same general process, many people also tend to assume that, in nature generally, a series of percepts following one another in time in the same context must constitute a chain of cause-and-effect. They say, for instance: first the root, then the shoot, then the flower — therefore the root is the cause of the flower.

In the case of the animal, the concept is 'built into it.' The squirrel and the nut are, as it were, part of the same process, adapted to each other so that the squirrel has no actual consciousness of the process, still less any concept of 'purpose' in it. The 'built-in concept' itself produces the animal's perceptual nature, and so decides its pattern of behaviour. We say that the bee acts 'from instinct,' but this is what instinct really implies.

When we realize this, we can better see what the human being has to do in order to produce an action. This process, by means of a mental picture, is necessary and right in us, but it applies to us alone amongst all creatures. God works through the gradual incarnation of ideas, which is what constitutes evolution. The ideas are, in themselves, the reality which is in, for example, the animal, and the appearance of a new species is the incarnation of a fresh idea. The idea is incarnated not only into the animal itself but also into its surroundings: thus, a cat is incarnated not only into its little body, but, as it were, permeates the house, which 'belongs to it,' and in which it can be aware of what is happening in another room. There is an *aim* in evolution, that is, the ideas which have not yet incarnated. God has an aim with us, because we are not yet finished, but we still cannot speak of a 'purpose' in the human sense. There is a lot of the idea connected with the human being which has not yet come down: therefore, we are not finished, but the animal is already fully incarnated, the whole idea has been 'built into it,' and it is finished. The idea 'monkey' was in the mind of God and this idea incarnated not merely in the monkey but in the environment connected with and necessary for its existence, the nuts, the trees and so on. The monkey is really not fully complete without this essential environment, and a monkey in a cage at the zoo can easily be felt to be incomplete. But we cannot say, by analogy with human thought-processes, that God 'thought out the monkey in order to fill a gap in the scheme of things.'

In the same way, history depends, not on a 'plan' in the human sense, but on the incarnating of ideas. And it depends on human beings whether these ideas incarnate properly. Take the case of Joan of Arc, who was approached by the Archangel Michael and told what she ought to do to drive the English out of France. The idea of the separation of France and England was to be incarnated through her, but she was not compelled to carry out her part of the process. Had she failed to do so, of course, it is possible that the same opportunity might have been offered to some other human being.

The difference between a 'plan' and the incarnating idea is one of method: a plan requires a mental picture and that percept and concept, originally separated, shall be brought together again, but with the world-all the percept and concept are never separated. The parts of the whole are all brought about simultaneously, and we cannot speak of a 'means to an end.' Human beings have to achieve their ends by means of planning, but with God the idea gradually incarnates and evolves — as a whole.

The free spirit is the one who makes a decision out of his own relationship with the spiritual world of ideas, and applies these, as a result of his own thinking, to the circumstances. In the course of the process he has to transform his apprehension of the idea into a mental picture. The unfree person accepts an already-existing mental picture, whether his own or one taken from someone else, or perhaps one which he considers to be in accordance with the will of God, but without going up to the spiritual world. When someone is acting out of freedom, he is making an absolutely original decision, in a situation which is unique and which will never again happen in quite the same form. The resulting action may be the same in either case, but the process is different. The decision cannot be thought out in advance, for the situation must be there first. In order to reach a free decision, we have to overcome our own characterological predisposition, and also the tendencies in our own nature which would hinder us from accepting the idea.

The relationship between the idea in the spiritual world and the decision taken is somewhat the same as that between the 'idea of a lion' and the actual, individual lion. We do not expect this single lion to be 'all lions,' but the 'idea of a lion' is universal. The ideas in the spiritual world are universal moral ideas, and in order to grasp these to bring them down we must use moral imagination. This moral imagination allows us to grasp enough of the idea to form a mental picture suitable for the situation, and this may enable us to come to a suitable decision. Such a free action is creative because it brings new, 'fresh' morality into the world, whereas the application of a principle, the acceptance of authority, is merely the re-use of stale, 'canned' morality. Only those who are endowed with moral imagination are, properly speaking, morally productive.

But it is still necessary to apply my individual decision to the world outside, and many a 'good' decision has gone wrong by being wrongly applied. We have to learn the facts of the situation, and then incarnate the decision into the situation in such a way that it bears worthy fruit, so as to transform the situation, the 'world of percepts,' without going contrary to the natural laws with which this is connected. The ability to do this is 'moral technique.' Many a reformer has produced unexpected, even disastrous results by wrongly, or too quickly, incarnating ideas excellent in themselves, in a way not adapted to the circumstances. This error may be in timing, in the language in which the idea is presented, or merely in failure to realize the consequences. Thus, we may consider some of the undesirable results of the forcible liberation of the slaves in the Southern States of America. Usually, what is wrong is not that these people are 'before their time' — an explanation often put forward when a projected reform wholly or partly fails — but that their 'moral technique' was wrong.

We are not equally developed in all our capacities, and may have unequal senses of moral imagination and of moral technique. Hence, it is possible for people whose moral imagination is weak to receive moral mental pictures from others, and to apply these in the world with success. Thus the complete process may have to be shared by two or more, human beings, one bringing down the idea and the other turning this into action.

What often happens is that we do not sufficiently study the circumstances into which the decision has to be incarnated, but give too much thought to our characterological predisposition, to our own feelings, or to the feelings of others. Our temperament is a part of what we have to overcome in order that we shall act out of freedom. Nor must we wonder what other people will think, for this can divert us from the actual circumstances and a calm study of these. Moral technique has to be, and can be, learned, but only when we can free our minds from our own personal angle can we really do what is right for the situation.

We can now connect these thoughts with the idea of evolution, which is generally accepted as being concrete evidence of 'purpose' in nature. Darwin expresses his Theory of Evolution as a chain of cause-and-effect, with earlier species producing later, more highly developed, ones. Historically, of course, we can look back on the whole process, arrange the species in chronological order, and observe 'evolution' in the course of time. While it is possible that a being whose span of existence covered a sufficiently long time might observe some of the actual changes taking place, we cannot imagine such a being,

standing at the time-stage when the fish was the highest creature existing, being able to 'think the monkey out of the fish'
by any process of reasoning or planning! Historically, looking
back from our present point of time, we can say, in retrospect,
that 'the monkey has evolved from the fish,' but it would be
impossible, with no percept more 'advanced' that that of the
fish, to form any concept of the monkey.

A morally creative human being is bringing something new
into the world. His idea is related, of course, to the ideas of
others who have gone before, but are not directly evolved from
these by any process of 'cause-and-effect.' The free human
being is creatively evolving something new, just as, on a higher
plane, God has evolved the world by a constant infusion of
new ideas from the spiritual world. Some of these (as with
some moral ideas) are lost or not properly fulfilled: some animal species are known to have died out very quickly, while the
creative idea of 'liberty, equality, fraternity' which underlay the
French Revolution was lost in savagery. But every human
being who does a free action is doing something creative, co-
operating, in the human sphere, with the spiritual world. If
such an action is not 'moral,' it can miscarry, but if it is moral it
can be compared with God's creation of a new animal species.
If such ideas miscarry, they can only return at other 'karmically
possible' times (not just at the next time when somebody
wants them), and then in a form changed to suit the changed
circumstances holding good at this later time.

Freedom in Relationships

We may now consider moral imagination from another angle, by means of the question of the value of life, 'whether life is worth living,' which was a deep philosophical problem of the latter part of the nineteenth century, though on a much less practical and pressing plane than that on which such a question would be asked today. This approach allows us to get a new idea of the ultimate importance of moral imagination to the human being.

On the one side, we have the optimists, exemplified by Shaftesbury and Leibnitz. The latter affirms that this world, having been created by a good, wise God, must be the best of all possible worlds. All that we need do is to find out the counsels of God and follow these. If we do not feel this, it must be our fault, not God's. There is no freedom here.

On the other side are the pessimists, exemplified by Schopenhauer and Eduard von Hartmann. Much more space is given to these in Chapter 12 of *The Philosophy of Spiritual Activity,* not because their arguments and conclusions are good but because out of these arguments we can advance to see the real value of moral imagination — something which von Hartmann would not admit and could not realize.

Schopenhauer thinks that the foundation of the world rests, not on a wise, beneficent being, but on blind will, eternally striving for a satisfaction which is beyond its reach, so that our whole lives consist of unsatisfied craving, dissatisfaction, and hence suffering. We have therefore according to him, a choice between continuing on this everlasting treadmill and stifling all desire and will. But the result of this would be universal boredom, a life without content, complete inactivity. It is hard to see how Schopenhauer was able to live his life to the end if he really believed all this.

Eduard von Hartmann approaches the problem from quite a different angle, and attempts to use his pessimism as a basis for great moral uplift and endeavour. He purports to base his world outlook on experience, to draw up a reasoned balance sheet of pleasure and pain in life, so as to discover which predominates: he decides that, though 'life would be worth living' if it gave us more pleasure than pain, the reverse is actually the case. But this pain, he considers, is no more then the pain of God himself, for the life of the world itself is identical with the life of God, whose purpose is to gain release from his own pain by the ending of all existence! Since, then, (according to von Hartmann) all life is pain, we should take no interest in pleasure (which would elude us anyway), but should give ourselves up to doing the will of God, who created the world as an outlet for his own suffering. If we work in a highly moral way, we shall help bring the world to an end, and so release God from his misery. Thus, there is no reason why we should go on living except high-minded devotion, a duty as external as that of Kant. Again, there is no freedom here.

In fact, of course, we do not draw up this sort of rational balance-sheet in life, nor do we live out of reason in von Hartmann's sense. But the interesting aspect of his point of view is that in it we have a chance to see how we actually do experience the value of living. Von Hartmann overlooked the essential point. He attached the pleasure and pain to the objects which we do or do not attain, to the drink or the ice-cream, the resulting hangover or stomach-ache. But, in fact, we relate the pleasure and the pain to something inside ourselves. We have a surplus of life-energy over our life-content, so that we are never satisfied with what we have, whether on the material plane or on a higher level, in spiritual matters. We always have the impulse to add to our content, and we experience the pleasure and pain on account of the process, not because of the things. The effort is not in itself painful: the pleasure or pain arises as a result of the proportion we attain, or do not attain, of what we hoped for. We are pleased or displeased in proportion as we attain, or fail to attain, the object. The life-energy is always directed to a particular end, which works back on the impulse. The pleasure in the anticipation of eating cake lies in ourselves, not in the cake — for we can find no such pleasure during a bilious attack. The pleasure, or pain, arises out of the way in which the impulse is achieved.

It may be objected that the object, when gained, may not prove worthwhile, with resulting disappointment. If I buy a wonderful looking cake, this may prove, on being eaten, to be a complete disappointment, but the pleasure of anticipation felt while buying it has not been done away with by the subsequent displeasure at finding it stale and tasteless. Indeed, the very disappointment over this cake may actually increase the anticipatory pleasure felt over the next one. It is to be noted, too, that in spite of his remarks about the hangover after a party more than compensating for the previous pleasure neither von Hartmann nor, generally, any other party-goer seems to think that he would be foolish to indulge in another party.

Von Hartmann then gives the example of an ambitious man who obtains a public honour which he has coveted and which gives him pleasure, but who later realizes that this is only pomp and empty show, which — so von Hartmann says — will destroy his pleasure. But in fact, even if he does realize the emptiness of the honour, he will not have lost the former pleasure which he felt at the time of gaining it, while his pain on realizing its emptiness may well be balanced by a new pleasure as he realizes that he has, himself, reached a higher level and a new wisdom, in that he has seen the emptiness of vanity. Von Hartmann fails either to see this or to allow for it.

We find that the process of impulse and attainment is fundamental for the human being. What interests us is what we are aiming at: if the interest is strong enough, we do not notice what we go through in the quest, while if we do, if we begin to find displeasure in these efforts, it is merely a sign that the interest is waning. This need not take place only in the material sphere: the same process is what gives value to life at all levels. The moral value arises when we can see an aim by the use of moral imagination and find sufficient enthusiasm for it, out of ourselves, to enable us to face whatever we have to go through in order to attain it. And the strength of the enthusiasm will depend on how far we have grasped the idea.

Von Hartman believed only in pleasure and pain, to be overcome only by devotion to the will of God, by duty to something outside ourselves, whereas moral imagination allows the human being, out of himself, to see some ideal, in the attainment of which he can then act as a free, individual spirit. The highest form of morality does not come about if we think of a duty imposed on us and then set out to have no pleasures of our own. Many people think that true self-sacrifice consists in the stifling of our own pleasures. But, if we grasp an aim with moral imagination and follow it, we shall gain great spiritual pleasure in doing so, nor should we stifle this pleasure instinct. We should rather increase it, but at the same time raise it to a higher level. Kant and von Hartmann would have us stifle our own desires; they would have us give up all impulses of our own to follow the will of God, seen as something external. But moral imagination becomes the organ of consciousness by which we can apprehend the will of God, unite ourselves with it, and then gain pleasure from doing it. The human mind becomes the friend, not the servant, of the spiritual world.

This view, of course, applies only to those people who actually do decide out of moral imagination, and not at all to those who are merely following their 'characterological predisposition' and thus following their selfish desires. The overcoming of this disposition is a first essential, so that the image can be grasped and brought down, uncoloured by and free of the disposition. The predisposition must, of course, be used for incarnating the idea into action, but it must not be allowed to make or influence the decision, which must be made out of moral imagination. We must not, of course, try altogether to stifle the predisposition, but we must keep it at a sufficient distance from the spiritual idea to prevent it from stifling or distorting this. A strong aim will usually allow us to overcome it to a sufficient extent.

We should note that our talents and strengths, as well as our weaknesses and faults, belong to our predisposition. But a common form of frustration today is that we are discouraged from doing something we could do well or something in which we are interested. moral imagination may lead us to abstain from doing something good in order to produce something better. This needs the conviction that the possession of the talent is not, in itself, a good reason for using it on all possible occasions. But we must use all our talents in order to implement the decision when this has been made.

From this point of view, the highest moral activity occurs when we become so independent of the 'characterological predisposition' that we can use moral imagination to contact the spiritual idea, bring this down into the sphere of mental pictures, and then find enough Moral Technique to carry it over into action. But we are all parts of groups, and it may be asked how we can act freely as individuals when there is so much group-nature in all of us. We must use this group-nature as part of our Moral Technique when carrying out the decision, but we must put it aside while bringing down the idea and forming the decision. We must not let the group-nature be our starting-point for this would not be acting out of freedom. We have to transcend the group-nature, whether this be nationality, family background, or anything else, so as to act through it but not out of it.

If one human being wants to meet the individuality of another (not just his personality of characterological predisposition), he must distinguish between these and realize that he can only meet the other's individuality in the sphere of his own freedom. He must penetrate to the innermost core of the other's being, and not stop short at what is merely 'typical.' He must use his own process of consciousness, which consists in bringing together percept and concept: we perceive the other in his individuality, but we must now hold back the concept of the other arising out of our own self, our judgment of the other, and take into ourselves, instead, the concepts by which the other determines himself, unmixed with the observer's conceptual content.

In ordinary social life, it is personalities which meet, not individualities. If we can take the other's concepts into ourselves, we can *know* him, recognize him for what he is and be in harmony with him, even though we may not agree with him. It is the personality which wishes to invade the other's being and to force its will on him: free individuals cannot interfere with one another. But this process of getting to know the other has to be carried out in the sphere of freedom, and the other must react out of this. Then, what happens may have great spiritual significance. If we have really found the other's individuality, the fruit of it may well appear rather in what he can say to us than in what we can say to him. This kind of knowledge of another leads to clear discernment and to tolerance: you may disagree but you do not want to interfere — nor are you taken in by the other's outward pose. It is a great help to him, even if you do not consciously let him know.

In this process, one is applying to another human being what one would otherwise apply in moral imagination to the spiritual world. A relationship is established in freedom and in the spirit, which releases us from any fear of having to live an individual 'hermit-existence,' which might have been aroused by last week's considerations.

23

Community out of Freedom

The last chapter of *The Philosophy of Spiritual Activity* is a recapitulation of the consequences of looking at things in the way
which has already been explained. If we look back over the
book, we see the two aspects of human life which, as it were,
divide the book into two parts: we see ourselves as human
beings who *know* and who *act*. We see the process by which the
human being who *knows* can open his mind to a new spiritual
idea, and how the human being who *acts* can open himself to a
new moral impulse from the sphere where morality is.
Though the sky over us is, as it were, a kind of closed roof, the
human being can go, with his thinking, through and beyond
this: though the created world around us is finished, the
human being can still bring something new into it, for his
power of thinking can reach up to the world of ideas, and thus
he can bring to the created world what is missing in it. This
created world was originally formed from the divine idea, but
it has now come to be only a copy of this idea: it can only come
back again to the actual idea when this shines out of the human
being. By making this possible, the human being can not only
bring something new into the created world, but he can also
make himself more truly human.

The greatest hindrance to the realization that thinking does
enable us to reach the objective world of ideas is the prejudice
that thoughts are given to us out of our sense-perceptions,
deduced from these as an abstract conception and not the
result of an independent activity of our own. We must free
ourselves from the mental picture that thinking is a mere

abstraction derived from reality, and not an independent reality in itself. The fact that we add our concept to the percept of, say, a tree, makes this complete. By the activity of thinking we actually add something to the world.

There is also the difficulty of distinguishing between the relative value of the content and of the process by which that content was reached. By the time that we have brought the idea into the sphere of mental picture the thoughts are no longer on the level from which they started: we have 'reduced them, and killed them off' in the process of thinking. It is not the content which makes the thought 'new,' but the process by which it has been produced, brought down anew from the world of ideas. For the activity of thinking is a truly spiritual activity, and the thought inevitably becomes a shadow of its original living self before it is formed in a human mind.

Thoughts stored in the mind tend, like food in a larder, to go bad unless we revive them by thinking the idea again. We can become just a bored, just as little roused to enthusiasm, by stale thoughts as by state bread. If we take a great, true thought — for example, a saying from the Gospels — and consider how many people have thought this and are still thinking it, we can nevertheless still add something to the stream of creative force which can flow through this idea if we 're-think' it instead of just using it 'ready-made.' The result will probably not show in what we can say about it, but in what others feel when we speak of it.

In a truly 'spiritual conversation,' the speaker should bring his hearer into his own connection with the idea, using as a percept the mental picture presented to him and bringing to this his own concept, derived from his own thinking. The process should not be at all like that of a bird feeding worms to its young, as it would be if we tried to push ready-made ideas into the other's mind. From the intellectual point of view, we can do this, but not from the spiritual point of view. We should try to put something between ourselves and the other which will be able to kindle his activity. We should not necessarily even present the whole picture, nor should we be for ever explaining: we should try to find an artistic, imaginative picture which will 'set him off.' From this picture, he can then feel the presence of the idea behind it. Too many explanations may have just the wrong effect, and set nothing off in the other.

The thing to be overcome is this muddle between the thoughts and the activity of thinking. A thought lives in the world in a different way according to how it has been born, though the content may seem to be the same. The clairvoyant is able to perceive how a rightly-born thought gives off a kind of spiritual light, how it benefits the created world. A thought which is coming into being is still a living thought: a 'thought thought' is already dead. But the fact that it has already once been reborn in us makes it easier for us again to 're-think' it in the future: it is here that the benefit lies, not in our having 'got a thought which is now ours for ever.'

We can see how, instead of being 'systematic' in his lectures, Rudolf Steiner used what appear like very roundabout methods. This enabled his hearers to follow him with their own creative activity. Certainly he prepared what he was going to say — it is quite wrong to look on him as almost a kind of 'medium' who simply stood up and let the spiritual world tell him what to say. He must have put an enormous amount of work into this preparation, but he was still able to reach the world of ideas while he was speaking, and to go off into apparent sidetracks in order to bring his hearers to the exact point from which the central idea could be seen from just the angle he required. We may notice the totally different mode of presentation of what appear to be the same basic ideas in some Theosophical writings.

If we can get over the difficulty of supposing that we derive the thoughts from our percepts, and can also distinguish between the thoughts and the process of thinking, our knowing ceases to be merely a process of enlightening our own minds, but it can become a process of actually bringing something new to the world: it can become of value to the world and not merely to ourselves. Most of us regard knowledge as, at most, something which we impart in a ready-made form to others, but if we can get out of this isolation and realize that our knowing is of value to the world, we can carry it into the sphere of the world and apply it to change the world. In an action which has moral imagination as its origin, we not only change the world but also bring into it a new creative force which would not otherwise be there. Whereas working with old thoughts is like moving the existing furniture to new positions in a room (and this may be seen in very many political 'thoughts' today), creative thinking is like bringing a new piece of furniture into the room. Another simile would be the difference between churning up the stale air in a room with an electric fan and opening a window to let in fresh air. moral imagination lets in fresh air.

The greatest hindrance to our letting moral fresh air into our deeds is the characterological predisposition. This causes us to act out of our own past instead of out of the present spirit. But if, as a human being, we can begin to use moral imagination, we find that not only can we produce a new situation but that at the same time we can become nearer to what a human being ought to be. As human beings, we are not yet 'finished,' and the means to bring ourselves to fulfilment is now in our own hands when we develop our own creative activity in moral imagination. There is no other creature on earth which has thus been left unfinished and then given the task of completing its own evolution for itself. The animals and plants have already become what was in their natures to be, and they are finished, but this is not the case with the human being. He has to finish himself. To use the process of consciousness which has been described in *The Philosophy of Spiritual Activity* is to fulfil ourselves as human beings, for the freely-acting human being is the air which lives in the mind of God. Nature has given us so much, and then has stopped: we should neither become civilized nor fully human by this alone. More is added by human society, by our education, background and so on, and this can make us 'civilized' — though it still cannot make us into 'fulfilled' human beings, a task which every individual must carry out for himself, by calling up in himself the spiritual possibilities of thinking and willing, and by really growing into these.

The human being does this from within, but the fact that he can do so at all depends on a force brought by Christ. Had Christ not come to earth, this could not have happened. This process of becoming free is the one by which the human being can lift himself up to become really human, using the Christ-given forces.

Most people today are not fully human. The tragedy of today is that so many people are trying to bring up old forces to solve present-day problems — as we may see in the resurgence of nationalism and in so-called 'ethnic cleansing.' The tendency is to call on old principles belonging to the characterological predisposition or to the race, instead of using individual creative activity. Behind this, we see a will to prevent evolution from going on.

The characterological predisposition naturally produces strife in the world: only creative activity produces love. But what we get from the predisposition can help us in Moral Technique, in incarnating our ideas into action. We can use the results of our past experiences (which have become part of our character), not in forming the decision (as many people consider they should) but in carrying this out: we must transform the predisposition, not cast it aside. Our talents should not be used as a reason for doing something 'just because I do it well' — this would interfere with our freedom — but these talents can be, and should be, used in carrying out the decision in the best way. We should so adjust the predisposition that instead of getting in the way it can be made useful to us in carrying our moral imagination over into action.

The human being when evolved to the next stage will not be a greater 'personality,' but he will be a greater individuality: thus, the personality will have to be adjusted. There will be no

need to fear that we shall all grow to be alike: the spiritual idea
will always enrich the world by entering it in a quite individual
way through every human being. Each of us says 'I' to himself
alone; we all use the same word, but no two of us mean the
same by it. The opposite tendency may be seen in the modern
trend to reduce people to mere 'numbers,' to common, unin-
dividualized units, to produce 'uniformity,' when all are to
think and feel and act alike.

The more individualized we become, the more freedom we
gain, the more we shall find what is common to us all. When
we see this, we shall realize that what is now usually called
'community' is very often little more than strife. But real unity,
which is not the same as uniformity, lies in the sphere of free
individuals. This kind of freedom is, at the same time, spiritual
love. With real unity, we are well aware that others think differently: we may disagree with their point of view, but if we
can realize that this arises from their free individuality we can
accept it without wishing to interfere. The other is 'being true
to himself.' When we can reach this kind of unity, we shall also
find harmony. There will no longer be the struggle of the one
to maintain himself against the other (which necessarily happens only too often in the physical sphere, though it should
not be carried over into the soul-sphere, into the sphere of
thought, as the characterological predisposition would like to
do). Every one of us will recognize the other. We shall be able
to realize that every one of us can still be 'honest,' though
holding different opinions, for what differs in these opinions
will represent various parts of the whole spiritual idea. For no
one of us can grasp the whole idea, and the part of this which
the other has grasped can add to my part of it. My existence is
confirmed, not threatened, by that of others. Through this
process of free, creative, individual intuitive thinking, the
human being not only fulfils himself but, in doing so, helps to
bring about real community.

Also by Evelyn Capel

The Christian Year

Advent, Christmas, Epiphany, Lent, Easter, Ascension, Whitsun, St John's, Michaelmas

The cycle of the Earth's changing seasons figures the eternal drama of life, death and resurrection. Waking and sleeping, breathing in and breathing out, humankind daily and annually lives through the cosmic rhythm together with the Earth itself and all of nature. The influence of sun, moon and other heavenly bodies affects every living thing.

Christianity reveals that it is cosmic in character through perpetuating the ancient observance of festivals throughout the year. Old traditions and customs do endure, though these are not easily comprehensible to many people nowadays. A new understanding is needed for the meaning of these festivals and a new appreciation for the spiritual rhythms in the life of the Earth. Then we shall discover for ourselves a bridge between the inner and outer life, along a path of truly Christian experience taking through each year.

Floris Books